Beginning Biblical Hebrew

BEGINNING BIBLICAL HEBREW

Intentionality and Grammar

Robert D. Sacks

Kafir Yaroq Books
Santa Fe, New Mexico

Manufactured in the United States of America

Kafir Yaroq Books
an imprint of Green Lion Press
Santa Fe, New Mexico
www.kafiryaroq.com
Set in 11-point New Baskerville.
Cover photograph by Hughes Leglise-Bataille:
View from Mt. Sinai at sunset, facing east.
Printed and bound by Sheridan Books, Inc.
Chelsea, Michigan
Cataloguing-in-Publication data:
Sacks, Robert D.
Beginning Biblical Hebrew: Intentionality and Grammar / by Robert D. Sacks
Includes index, bibliography, biographical note.

ISBN–13:   978–1–888009–33–0 (sewn softcover binding)
1. Biblical Hebrew. 2. Hebrew Grammar. 3. Intentional Grammar.
I. Sacks, Robert D., (1931–), II. Title

Library of Congress Control Number: 2008937594

Table of Contents

Dedication

This book is dedicated to two men: to the late Professor Joseph Rivlan of the Hebrew University of Jerusalem, and to Mr. Michael Ossorgin of St. John's College in Santa Fe, New Mexico. Though I believe myself to have learned much from both of them, in each case this dedication is made because of single sentence.

Once in an Arabic class Professor Rivlan mentioned to me that he thought the Hebrew word מדבר (medabber), the participle of the verb *to speak*, came from two Semitic roots, מן (man), which means *who* and דבר (dabar), which means *speaks*. I was deeply affected by his words. With this sentence, Professor Rivlan had transformed a dead linguistic form into a living thought, and I began to wonder if it might not be possible to use his insight in order to gain a fuller understanding of Hebrew grammar as a whole. The rest of this book is little more than a commentary on his thought.

In a discussion I had one day with Mr. Ossorgin, he claimed that Gregorian chant was falling music, whereas modern western music is rising music. At first the distinction did not make very much sense to me; but as I listened again, I could begin to hear what he meant. So far as I can tell from the musical notation in the biblical text, Mr. Ossorgin's distinction seems to be critical for Hebraic chant as well. At any rate, we shall see more of this in Chapter 13, which is deeply influenced by the words of that fine scholar.

There is one other matter which I must somehow manage to sneak beneath the radar of my two fine editors, Howard Fisher and Dana Densmore. That is to acknowledge their years of kind and rigorous dealing with this text, at first as students—guinea pigs, one is tempted to say—of the view of language that is embodied here. In the years that ensued they became in several respects my guides; and surely by now they have spent more critical hours poring over this text than did its author in writing it. I thank them for that.

1. The Beginning

Some books begin at the beginning. Euclid, for instance, begins with the definitions, postulates, and axioms of his science of Geometry, just as the Bible begins with the book of Genesis. But where is the beginning of language? If we do not know where language begins, how shall we know where we should begin? Modern writers on the subject tend to define language as an arbitrary set of symbols commonly agreed upon for the purpose of communication. But any definition of that sort would seem to be almost self-contradictory, since any such agreement would obviously presuppose some prior communication, leaving us with an infinite regress. The first users of language, then, must have had some reasons, no matter how vague, for believing that their words reflected some facet of the objects of their discourse, at least to the extent that their primitive speech would be intelligible to their addressees.

When, on the other hand, one looks at the myriad of languages spoken throughout the world and the depth of their differences not only in vocabulary but in their deep structure as well, any hint of the naturalness of language would seem to be no more than seventeenth-century poppycock. Still, the problem of the beginning continues to gnaw and to taunt. To study a language, then, is to enter that strange and foreboding land which lies somewhere between mathematical necessity and the totally arbitrary. It is that unknown land of grayness in which most of us live our daily lives.

As I recounted in the Dedication, the late Professor Joseph Rivlan once mentioned to me that he thought the Hebrew word מדבר (medabber), the participle of the verb *to speak*, came from the two Semitic roots מן (man), which means *who* and דבר (dabar), which means *speaks*. The participle, then, was once not just a grammatical form, but rather the meaningful phrase *he who speaks*. On the basis of this hint I began to consider the relationship between *grammatical form* and *intentionality*. As the derivative character of the forms became clearer, I began to wonder whether it was not possible to look at grammar from a purely *intentional* point of view rather than from the point of view of *formality*.

One way of beginning such a study would be to look at more ancient languages which are cognate to Hebrew, such as Babylonian and Assyrian; and indeed we will have to do just that. But first it will be desirable to see what kind of assistance we might thereby hope to gain.

Consider the teacher of a hypothetical dialect of the English language spoken some two thousand years hence, in which the words *wouldn't, shouldn't, didn't* and *couldn't* still exist, as well as the words *would, should, did* and *could*. Let us further suppose, however, that the word *not* had fallen into disuse several centuries earlier and was no longer in the memories of the speakers of that language. The teacher, then, would have two possible ways of explaining the language. As a first approach, he might give his students a rule according to which certain words may be negated by adding the symbols *n't*. Such an approach would not differ in any way from giving the kind of rule we learn today, for example that the plural of most words is formed by the addition of the letter *s*.

The other way would be to point to the ancient word *not* and allow the students to see that *couldn't* is a mere contraction of the words *could* and *not*. According to the second approach, then, what first appeared to be a *formal* aspect of language was actually an *intentional* factor.

The importance of such considerations can be seen more clearly by considering a word such as *slowly*. Originally, it was a mere contraction of the phrase *slow like*, as can still be seen in the corresponding Germanic ending *-lich*. But in time, as people became more at home with the abstract, the contraction became a word in itself and the very sophisticated notion of an adverb came to be. The question then arises as to whether our sophistication is not somewhat false if we do not see the actual abstraction taking place before our own eyes.

One might imagine a child born into a world in which abstract art had so taken over the field that the child would no longer be aware of the possibility of representational art. Like those islanders who, we are told, cannot recognize a picture as a picture, the child might find Rembrandt's self-portrait a beautiful and well-balanced combination of colors—no more and no less.

No longer thinking of the possibility of representing the world by means of pictures, the child would no longer understand abstract art as touching the heart of that world from which it had once been abstracted; it would have become a beautiful, but meaningless, form.

Intentional grammar is not and cannot become a subject matter. It cannot be taught; a book can do no more than invite the reader to participate in the activity. Intentional grammar is most at home spreading out like a fog in the low valleys between the great peaks of historical grammar and linguistics. It has no interest in the dead past, but it often finds itself unable to distinguish the living present from the dead past. Too often it finds formal grammar to be a realm of ghosts wearing the clothes of living men. The forms have been well-defined, but they prove themselves to be no more than mantles draped over thoughts which have and have not been thought for thousands of years. These ancestral thoughts which we inherit, not through any collective unconsciousness but through words and half-meaningful turns of speech, must be rethought in order that our own might become our own. Often, to see them born means to see them naked, devoid of their formalistic clothing.

The reader will find this introduction to the Hebrew language a bit erratic. At times it will belabor small points in order to exhibit the process more fully. At other times it will give only the slightest indication of the meaning and depth of a word, inviting the reader to continue the activity unassisted. Often, for instance, the dictionary definition of a noun will be replaced by a simple reminder that the reader has already learned a cognate verb, since part of our endeavor will be to re-think the position of the person who possessed the verb and needed the noun. For this reason, we shall need some overall picture of what are known as the Semitic languages.

One important fact to bear in mind is that the Semitic languages form a much more closely interrelated group than do the Indo-European languages. It would be appropriate to think of the Semitic languages as comparable the Romance languages in terms of their proximity. The Semitic languages can, however, be broken down into two major groups, Eastern Semitic and Western Semitic. If speakers of an Eastern Semitic and a Western Semitic language were to attempt conversation, each would sense that the other's language was related to his own, and each might even catch many of the other's words. But they would not be able to understand one another's speech; their relationship would be rather like that of a Frenchman to an Italian.

The Eastern Semitic language, called Akkadian, was written in *cuneiform*, a method of writing developed by the non-Semitic Sumerians and taken over by the Akkadians around the year 2000 BCE. It was spoken by two different peoples and soon evolved into two readily distinguishable dialects, Babylonian in the South and Assyrian in the North. Each dialect went through certain periods of change, shown in Table 1.1.

Old Babylonian	2000–1800 BCE
Old Assyrian	2000–1500
Middle Babylonian	1500–1000
Middle Assyrian	1500–1000
Literary Babylonian	1400–500
Late Assyrian	1000–600
Late Babylonian	600–1

Table 1.1

The Western Semitic languages, on the other hand, break down into two major groups, the Northwest and the Southwest. The Northwest, which had been all of a piece, called Ugaritic, then split into two branches in the eighteenth century BCE. The relationship between these Northwestern languages is more like that between Spanish and Italian than between Italian and French, since with sufficient care, people who spoke these two different languages could probably have conversed with one another. Canaanite Hebrew, along with Phoenician and Moabite, which are all nearly identical, together form one of these branches. The other branch of Ugaritic came to be called Aramaic. It was spoken in Damascus and in the surrounding countryside known today as Syria and Lebanon. The Southwestern Semitic language consists primarily of Arabic and Ethiopian.

Languages change in strange ways, and often the most corrupt language can preserve the most ancient forms. In general, our work will lead us to consider Babylonian and Northern Arabic, since they tend to preserve the more ancient ways of speaking. They are a strange pair, since Babylonian was one of the first of the Semitic languages to be committed to writing, whereas Arabic was one of the last. In the one case, antiquity was preserved for us under a pile of rubble and brush; in the other, by a nomadic people without a written tongue. In the case of our own language, matters seem to have fallen out the other way. Shakespeare and the King James Bible have considerably slowed down the rate of English's linguistic change, whereas Akkadian began to change and lose its form quite soon after it was committed to writing,

Although *language* primarily means spoken language, our only access to the Hebrew language of the Bible is through the written word. Fortunately, fairly much is known about the beginning of writing, though the path is by no means uniformly clear. The Ancients said that the Greeks received the art of writing from the East, and that it had been brought to them by a man named Cadmus. The depth of this myth we shall be able to face only in the next chapter. For the moment it is sufficient to note that the name Cadmus is of Semitic origin, and it has the double meaning of both *ancient* and *east*. The Ancients also agreed that Cadmus did not invent the art of writing but received it from another people. According to Plato, he received it from the Egyptians, but according to Plutarch he received it from the Syrians. Ours is a century of modern science rather than a century of myth, but the argument continues and, as we shall see in the next chapter, some modern scholars derive the Phoenician alphabet from the Egyptian hieroglyph, whereas others favor the Assyrian cuneiform. Although the precise generation of the Phoenician alphabet is still unknown, modern scholars have indeed discovered an impressive amount concerning the kind of thing that must have taken place.

Writing was conceived along with art and science in a dark cave when the first person realized that it was possible for a little thing to look like a big thing (Figure 1.2). It might sound contradictory to say that thought has its beginnings in a lie, and yet to grasp an image *as* an image means seeing a thing as somehow being what it is not. Some early people must have become fascinated by the fact that a bit of charcoal and less than a gram of sienna could have all the power and force of a wild buffalo charging over the plains. Others became fascinated by the fact that little things could be made to look *precisely* like big things. Eventually they went on to draw plans for buildings, and finally some became totally absorbed in the awesome clarity of relationships between their precise lines; these people went on

Figure 1.2. Cave painting, Lascaux, France

to become geometricians. We shall be interested, however, in those who realized that by means of their simple scratchings a tale could be told.

2. The Origins of Writing

Written signs have a strange and almost contradictory way about them. When looked at in themselves, they appear to be completely arbitrary. Nothing could be simpler than for an author to assign any meaning he wished to any sign invented by him or by another. And yet this rarely happens; the human mind does not work in that way. Words all have their etymologies, and even the alphabet has an ancient history. This holds true even in relatively modern times. Our plus sign (+) was once the letter *t*, and originally just shorthand for the Latin word *et*. Our minus sign (–) was once a wavy line (~), and if one goes back far enough, one finds that it was just the letter *m* standing for the word *minus*. Similarly, our equal sign (=) was once no more than the Latin symbol æ for *aequale*.

All of us have had occasion to write ourselves little notes with funny symbols meant for our eyes alone. And yet in each case there is always at least a hint of human reflection in the shape of our marks. This was no less true in the beginning.

It is difficult to know why people began to draw pictures. At first, or so it would seem, they mingled their hopes, fears, and memories with a wall. The markings were intended as reminders of what was—of a big hunt, perhaps. The whole story was held in common by the artist and the wall; each was lost without the other. Later, however, these pictures developed a life of their own and messages could be sent. Thoughts which were present to the mind of a particular person at a certain time and in a certain place could be hacked into cold hard stone, only to come alive again in the mind of another person in another time and in another place. We find a rather sophisticated example of this practice as late as the nineteenth century in the letter sent by a Cheyenne named Turtle-Run-After-His-Wife written to his son Little-Man at Pine Ridge (Figure 2.1). Upon receiving the note, Little-Man immediately went to the Pine Ridge agent to ask for the fifty-three dollars that his father had mentioned in the letter, and then Little-Man returned home as requested.

Figure 2.1. Cheyenne Indian Letter (undated; from Mallery, 1893)

No writing of such immediate intelligibility has ever been found in the caves of the Middle East. If such comparable stages existed, all traces of them have been lost; the earliest writings found there date from what must be a much later period. In the meantime there had transpired a foreshadowing of the Cartesian Revolution, in which insight and quick wit had given way to schools and methodology. The signs had become rigid, and now only those who had spent many years in training knew the art of writing. At the same time analogues had taken over. A picture of a foot, for instance, no longer represented only a foot, but now represented the act of walking as well. Similarly, the sun could represent not only itself, but could denote *one day*; so that two suns could represent two days, though no one had ever actually seen two suns at the same time.

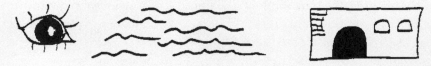

Above is a highly simplified example of the next type of writing we are to consider. It is intended to mean *I see the house,* but from this made-up example the reader can begin to see why years of schooling might be required in order to learn the art of writing in this more complex form.

Note the three major changes that have taken place. First of all, this writing communicates the precise words of the author rather than a general idea, as had been the case in the Cheyenne letter. Second, all of it must be read in one direction only. Finally, most important of all, it can be read only by someone who speaks the English language.

The next stage in the development of language might be represented by the following symbols:

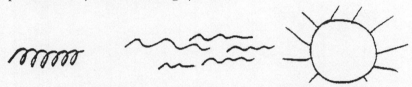

To anyone who had become familiar with this way of writing, this would have meant *spring season*. Note that the wavy lines no longer represent the sea. They now represent only the syllable *see*, which can now be combined with other symbols to make whole words.

A further stage might have looked something like this:

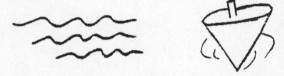

As one would have learned in the schools of Egypt, this was not to be read as *sea top*, but *stop*. Perhaps with the passage of time, and through familiarity, people would have begun to replace the several horizontal wavy lines with a single, vertical, wavy line, thus writing this word *stop* as 𝗦⏛; and so we might imagine the birth of the letter *S*.

These examples have been contrived for the English-speaking reader, but Egyptian hieroglyphs worked in just such a manner. In fact, our letter *m* may have had a very similar origin and probably goes back to the Semitic sign for the root *ma'a*, meaning *water*.[1] While the hieroglyphic writers did, in fact, produce what we today might be tempted to call letters, they were still complicated signs, such as pictures of eagles and ducks. Moreover, they were no more than a minor part of writing and were primarily used merely to indicate grammatical endings.

---

1. Much of the following discussion of the origins of the alphabet follows the treatment given in G. R. Driver, *Semitic Writing*.

| Hiero-glyph | EGYPTIAN | | | SEMITIC | | | | |
	Word	Meaning	Value	Phoenician Signs	Arabian Signs	Name	Meaning	Value
⌓	id	hand	d	2? ?Z	ꟼ b	yod	hand	y
◯	ri	mouth	r	))))	⊙⊙ᴍ	pe	mouth	p
Y	zhn-t	prop	—	Y Y Y Y	⊙ ▽	waw	peg	w
∿∿∿	n-t	water	n	ᒲ ᒲ ᒲ ᒲ	↕ ⍵	mem	water	m
✝	(?)	(?)	—	✗ ✗ ✝	✗ ✝	taw	mark	t
))	qmi	throw-stick	—	⌐ ∧ ⌐	⌐ ⌐ ∧	gimel	throw-stick	g
⟶	zun, zhn	arrow	—					
⟶•	?	bolt	z	I I I	ᴴ T	zayin	weapon (?)	z
⌂	?	folded cloth	s					
Θ	ip	head	—	ꟼ ꟼ ꟼ ꟼ	))	reš	head	r
⟶	irt	eye	—	⊙	⊙	ayin	eye	'(ʿ)
▯	ei	door	—	◁ ◁	↕ ↕	dalet	door	d
⫰	ki	ox	—	K K K	▽▽K	alep	ox	'(ʾ)
↘	hni	rush	—	∨ ∨ ∨	⌁	kap	hand, bough	k
∽∽	his-t	hill-country	—	w w w̄	) {	šin	tooth, peak	š
⎰	eu-t	peasant's crook	—					
↑	hqi	crooked staff	—	ꞁ ꞁ ꞁ ꞁ	ꞁꞁꞁꞁ	lamed	goad	l
ꟿ	wis	sceptre	—					
⊓	h	courtyard	h	ꟼꟼ ꟼꟼ	⊓⊓ ⊂	bet	house	b
⊲	in-t	bulti-fish	—	⅂ ⅂	ꟿ	samek	fish (?)	s
⌇	wid-t	cobra	—	5 5 ꟼꟼ	ꟼꟼ ꞁ5	Aram. nun fish / Eth. nahas serpent		n
✗	q i / hei / he	high / rejoiced / mourner	—	ꟼ ꟼ ꟺ ꟺ	ꟼ ⅄	he	lo!	h
⫯	h	twisted hank	ḫ	ꓮꓮ ꓮꓮ	⊓ ꟺ	het	—	ḥ
			—	⊕	◫	tet	—	t
		grasshopper	—⌋	ꞁ ⌐ ⌐	ꞁ	ṣade	cricket	s
		monkey	—⌋	φ φ	φ	qop	monkey (?)	q

Figure 2.2. Affiliation of Egyptian and Semitic Alphabets (from Driver)

Occasionally, one does find whole words spelled out with these "letters," but such words usually turn out to be foreign names that could not be dealt with in the normal manner. Even then, they could not stand on their own as words should. The name *Cleopatra,* for instance, could be spelled out, but it would have to

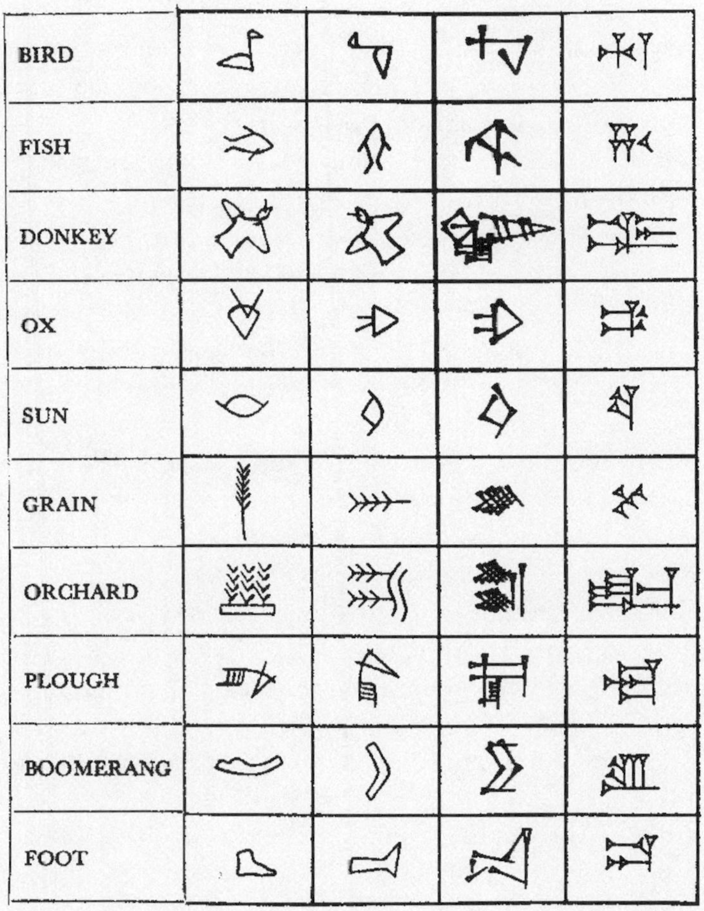

Figure 2.3. Development of Cuneiform shapes (from Gelb)

be enclosed within the symbol meaning *ruler* and followed by the symbol meaning *feminine.*

As can be seen in Figure 2.2, some modern scholars believe that the Phoenician and early Hebrew alphabets—which are very closely related—can be traced back to these signs. The argument in favor of the hieroglyphic origin of these alphabets is, however, not nearly so clear as one might think by looking at the chart. The Egyptian scribes were by no means in agreement as to which sign should be used for which letter. Even the same scribe would often use different signs for the same letter, and it is clear enough that we often see what we wish to see, given enough places in which to look. Nevertheless, I find the argument fairly persuasive even though it is far from being universally accepted.

At the same time the Babylonians were also developing a somewhat similar kind of writing; but rather than chipping words onto stone they scratched them into tablets of clay and then baked the tablets. It was soon discovered that one could get a cleaner line by using a triangular stylus and pressing it into the clay in different directions, rather than scratching the surface. The development of these symbols can be seen in Figure 2.3.

The Babylonians never developed anything that could properly be called a letter. Instead, they developed syllables. *Bo* was represented by one symbol, *Ba* by a completely different symbol, and *Ab* by a third. Some scholars believe that they have found in these symbols the origins of our alphabet.

Whatever their actual sources, the Phoenicians would have had to do a great deal of work in order to convert them into a true alphabet. The Egyptian "alphabet," if one may even call it such, was at best a makeshift and uncomfortable way of dealing with the problem of foreign names. It must have taken someone from the outside to see in that uncomfortable situation the seeds of a general solution. The alphabet, unlike earlier forms of writing, had to emerge like Athena—full grown from the head of a single person, mortal or immortal—since its parts are useless without the whole.

Figure 2.4 shows the common origins of the Greek, Latin, English, and Hebrew alphabets. The art of writing began around the ninth century BCE. As one can see, the Hebrew alphabet as we know it today was pretty well formed by the tenth century CE in Babylon.

Because early Semitic writing was carried out with hammer and chisel, the natural direction was from right to left, with the chisel held in the left hand and the hammer in the right. The Semitic languages generally preserved the right-to-left direction; but when the Greeks adopted alphabetic writing, pen and ink had already become widespread. Greek and Latin writing reversed course, presumably so as not to smear the still-drying letters.

Notice that when writing changed direction, the individual letters went to their mirror images, while some became turned on their sides. Bearing this in mind, it is not too hard to see how the Greek and Latin letters developed from them. While the Greek, Latin, and English alphabets still noticeably resemble the early Hebrew alphabet, the alphabet of modern Hebrew has undergone a more extensive shift.

Greek	Latin and English	Early Hebrew and Aramaic	Aramaic			Aramaic and Hebrew Square character	Hebrew	
		8 cent. BCE	8-7 cent. BCE	5-4 cent. BCE	5-3 cent. BCE	Early inscr. 1-1 cent. CE	Baby-lonian 916 CE	Machine printed 19 cent.
A α	A a							
B β	B b							
Γ γ	C c							
Δ δ	D d							
E ε	E e							
Ϝ	F f							
Z ζ	G g							
H η	H h							
Θ θ								
I ι	I i							
K κ	K k							
Λ λ	L l							
M μ	M m							
N ν	N n							
Ξ ξ								
O o	O o							
Π π	P p							
ϡ								
Ϙ	Q q							
P ρ	R r							
Σ σ	S s							
T τ	T t							
Υ υ	V v (Latin) / U u (English)							

Figure 2.4. Development of Greek, Latin, and Hebrew Alphabets
(adapted from Gesenius)

As Figure 2.4 shows, the Greek α and the Early Hebrew ✦ are very nearly the same shape. The Early Hebrew ⊅ closed up the bottom circle when it turned around and became B in both Greek and Latin and in English. Similarly one can discern both C and Γ in the Early Hebrew ⌐, and in fact the Latin name Caesar was probably once pronounced Gaesar. However, in later times the G-sound that was originally associated with C softened to the K-sound; and in some cases it softened even further—first to a Ch-sound, and finally to the S-sound that C sometimes has in English. As we also see, the Early Hebrew ⅀ became the vowel E in Greek, Latin, and English, while ५ became Greek Ϝ (digamma) and Latin and English F. Similarly, ⌷ became the Greek vowel H (eta), while in Latin and English it became the consonant H.

The Early Hebrew letter that was written either ⊥ or ⊇ was pronounced Z. It developed into the Latin G and ultimately came into English as our soft G. To hear the shift in sound, think of the English word *azure*. Early Hebrew ⊕ became Greek Θ.

The remaining letters should be pretty clear, but note that Early Hebrew ⅄ was turned on its head to make K while others, like ⱳ and ✗, were turned on their sides to become Σ (sigma) and T (tau) in Greek, while in Latin and English they became S and T. It is said that when Cadmus brought writing to the Greeks, he invented the letter Υ—forerunner of Latin V—while watching a flock of wild cranes in flight.

While the Greek, Hebrew, and Latin and English alphabets generally resemble one another in sound as well as shape, in this chapter we have been concerned mainly with the relationships among the shapes of the letters.

3. What is a Letter?

All the letters of the Hebrew alphabet stand for some pronounceable sound. This is not true of English letters, as you will recognize for yourself if you try to pronounce the first letter in the word *boat*. We do, of course, make a feeble attempt to pronounce the letter by a sound which may be represented as *buh* or *b'*. This, however, is not quite satisfactory, since we say *boat* and not *buh-oat*. The Hebrew equivalent to the English letter *B* is ב. but the Hebrew letter ב is a full sound, either *ba* or *bi* or *bu*; whereas the English letter *B* requires a vowel along with it in order to be heard. Similarly, the equivalent to our *D* is ד, which might be pronounced *da, di* or *du*.

When Hebrew letters are combined into a syllable they are regarded as sharing equally in their pronounceable quality. For example, בד might have been pronounced *bad* (or *bid* or *bud*), while דב might have been *dab*; in both cases the ב continues to stand for a full sound, whether it begins the syllable (as *ba*) or ends it (as *ab*).

As we shall see later, the most primitive form of the Semitic languages probably used only the *A* mode of pronunciation. That is to say, they would only have had the syllables *ba* and *bad*. But quite early in the development of the language, the syllables *bid* and *bud* (sounded *bood*) were added in order to give a slightly different nuance to the word. Much later, other possibilities developed, primarily because of certain shifts in the vocalic structure of the language.

Such an arrangement would certainly be chaos in English. Consider the syllable *bd*. It can be read as *bad, bid, bed, bud, bode, bide, bead, bade,* etc. In early Hebrew, however, the word could only be *bad*, which means *a piece of cloth*. An even more important contrast is that in English the vowels are an essential part of the root meaning of the word. Many of those eight English *bd* words have no etymological connection at all, whereas in Hebrew it is precisely what we would call the consonants that contain the root sense—the vocalic components determining only variations, howsoever important (and sometimes far-flung) they may be.

However, after the Babylonian Exile in the sixth century BCE, not all who could read Hebrew were fully proficient in it. Therefore, around the fifth century BCE a group of scholars in Tiberias, known as the Masoretes, invented a set of marks which enabled the reader to distinguish between the syllables *ba, bi,* and *bu.* Although we might be tempted to call these marks vowels, it is better to think of those signs not as having sounds in and of themselves, but as indicating how the letters which they accompany should be pronounced. Perhaps the Coptic scholars represented the situation somewhat more precisely. Rather than using additional marks, they indicated the vocalic mode by varying the shapes of their letters in a consistent way—as if B were to denote *ba* and D *da,* but *B* would be *bi* and *D di,* while B would be *bu,* and D du.

We are now in a position to take more seriously the myth of Cadmus. Two major changes took place in the development of the Greek alphabet. First, the direction of writing changed and, as one can see from Figure 2.5, that entailed a reversal in the direction of the individual letters themselves. The second change was much more radical. It was not possible to write Greek with the Semitic alphabet, because in Greek the vocalic sounds lead a life of their own and are not simply part of the mode in which the consonant is pronounced, as in the Semitic languages. Again, a new way of writing had to be established and that act had to be done at one blow. Certain of the Semitic letters that were no longer needed in Greek were converted into vowels. But to say so is to speak as if the concept of a vowel were clear, when quite the contrary was probably true. All that would have been apparent is that something was missing. In spite of the fact that *ba,* for example, is a single sound and had been represented by a single Semitic letter, writing the Greek language would have become intolerably complicated had not an artificial distinction been made between the *b* factor and the *a* factor. Cadmus—and if he had another name, why not call him Cadmus anyway?—not only had to see the need for vowels, but also had to make certain decisions about which letters should stand for which vowels. In some cases the choice was practically dictated by the situation, but in others an almost arbitrary choice had to be made. Such an integrated system, in which the parts are meaningless without the whole, can only be the work of a single mind.

In the present chapter, we shall spend what might seem to be a rather inordinate amount of time considering the pronunciation of each letter. This is necessary because Semitic grammar is far more dependent upon euphony than are most of the Indo-European languages—though it must be admitted that Greek, Sanskrit, and some others give it a good run for the money. The problem of euphony arises only occasionally in English; an example is the change which takes place in the indefinite article when we say *a book*, but *an apple*.

Even if we neglect the way our thoughts are reflected in our hands, in our eyes, and in the look in our faces, we translate our thoughts into speech through the use of a large number of parts of our body. First, we use the lungs and diaphragm to force air up through the windpipe. Not all languages consistently use the lungs. Some African languages use clicks, and some American Indian languages have sounds similar to our *P*, *T*, *K*, and *Ts*, but which are formed by using air which is trapped in the mouth and throat areas. But Hebrew, like English, uses only air from the lungs.

After leaving the windpipe, the air goes through a small chamber called the larynx, or voice box, which contains the vocal cords and the glottis. We can close off the stream of air by means of the lips, as in the case of the letters *B* and *P* (which are for that reason called *Bilabials*) or we can close off the stream of air by means of the glottis. This organ is not normally thought of as being used as an integral part of English speech, though it is often active. We know its action best from the way we have of cutting off the stream of air when lifting a heavy object. It also occurs in the English word *bottle* as it appears in the English Cockney dialect and is sometimes represented as *bo'l*. Actually, the glottal stop, for so it is called, often appears in standard English when we wish to avoid elision between vocalic sounds.

As the stream of air leaves the voice box, it can be diverted into the nose, producing sounds such as *M* or *N*, called the *Nasals*; or it can pass directly into the mouth cavity. If the teeth are interposed, a kind of hissing sound is produced, creating a group of sounds such as *S* or *Z*, called *Sibilants*; or, as we have noted before, the lips may be interposed, producing the *Bilabials* like *B* or *P*. A variant of this form can be produced by interposing the upper teeth and lower lip, as we do in pronouncing the letters *F* and *V*.

The other sounds that occur in English, and in Hebrew too, are produced by allowing the tongue to play against the roof of the mouth anywhere from the tip of the tooth to the back of the windpipe, producing such sounds as *T, R,* and *K.* These phoneme types have various names, and we shall see more of the particulars as we discuss the pronunciation of individual letters.

א *Aleph.* It is important to bear in mind that the *Aleph* is as much a letter—or, as we English-speaking people would be tempted to say at first glance, as much of a consonant—as the letters *B* or *K.* When producing the letter *B,* we close off the air stream with our lips and burst out into a vocalic sound. א is pronounced in a similar manner, but in this case the air stream is cut off by the glottis prior to the burst. The family of sounds that contains the glottal stop, *B, K,* etc. is known as the *Plosives.*

ב *Beth.* The fundamental sound of the letter *Beth* is produced by means of the same lip movements as is the sound of our letter *B* in the word *boat.* It is formed by stopping the air flow with the lips and allowing the sound to explode as the lips are parted. It differs from the letter *P* in that during its articulation, the vocal cords are brought together, placing them within the air flow so that they vibrate. When the vocal cords are so interposed, the sound is called *voiced* (for example, *B, D, G*). If the vocal cords are not interposed, the sound is called *unvoiced* (for example, *P, T, K*).

The letter *Beth* presents a difficulty which it shares with five other Hebrew letters. Since it is essentially an explosion, it cannot be pronounced as such at the end of a syllable. In English we avoid the problem by swallowing the sound, as in the word *tub.* In Hebrew the problem is avoided by leaving a small gap for the air to escape; thus in Hebrew, the word *tub* would be pronounced as if it had been spelled *tuv.* In transliteration we shall write it *tubh,* in order to maintain the kinship between *Bh, Kh* (pronounced like the *ch* in *Bach*), and *Th* (pronounced like the *th* in *thing*). These alternative sounds are called *Fricatives.*

The tendency to use the alternative pronunciations became more dominant in Hebrew and was ultimately used whenever the letter was approached from a vocalic sound. At the beginning of a word, though, or when following a syllable that ends in a consonantal sound, it is still pronounced as the letter *B.* Thus, one says *BaNiM* and *KaL-Bi,* but *La-BhaN* (pronounced *lavan*). However, if two words are felt to be connected, and the first ends in a vocalic mode, the second may begin with a fricative as in *'Elu BhaNiM.*

Since the fifth century BCE the two modes of pronunciation have sometimes been distinguished by placing a dot, called a *dagesh*, in the *Beth* (בּ) when it is to be pronounced as *B*, and leaving out the dot (ב) when it is to be pronounced *Bh*.

ג *Gimmel* is normally pronounced like the English letter *G*, as in the word *goat*. In order to describe it more accurately, it will be necessary to consider the roof of the mouth in greater detail. The roof of the mouth, called the hard palate, begins at the dental ridge where the teeth are implanted. Near the back of the mouth the roof becomes fleshy, and we enter a region known as the soft palate. Except for the trap door which leads into the nasal cavity, the roof of the mouth is continuous with the back of the windpipe. The letter *Gimmel* is a voiced *Palatal*; that is to say, it is formed by cutting off the flow of air by holding the back of the tongue against the soft palate and then letting go.

Since ג is a plosive, it obviously suffers from the problems discussed in the case of the letter בּ. In similar fashion, then, when ג was preceded by a vocalic sound, it was written ג and pronounced like the letter γ in modern Greek, or as the *R* of Parisian French. In modern times this pronunciation is seldom used, but one must bear it in mind in order to have a full understanding of a number of grammatical variations that we will come upon later.

ד *Daleth* is similar to the English letter *D*, but is pronounced a little differently. The English *D* is pronounced by curling up the tongue and allowing it to make full contact with the hard palate, completely sealing off the flow of air. The exact point of contact varies according to the sound which follows it; the *d* in *door* does not use exactly the same placement as does the *d* in *draft*. The Hebrew letter *Daleth*, which belongs to a family of letters called the *Dentals*, is always formed by placing the tip of the tongue on the ridge between the hard palate and the teeth, as in the diagram.

The *Daleth*, too, suffers from the problems mentioned in connection with *Beth* and *Gimmel*; and its alternate form ד, with no dagesh, is pronounced as the *th* in the English word *this*. Sadly, this nicety has also disappeared from modern pronunciation.

ה *He* is pronounced exactly as the English letter *H*. It is an unvoiced breath of air.

ו *Waw*. This letter was pronounced exactly as the English *W*. It is shaped by the lips, but the breath is allowed to pass freely; and for that reason, while it is one of the family of Bilabials, it also belongs to another group which we call *open*, and which also includes *He* and a few others. In modern times, however, it is generally pronounced as we would pronounce the letter *V*.

ז *Zayin*. This letter, pronounced like the English letter *Z*, is a voiced *Sibilant*.

ח *Ḥeth* belongs to a group of letters that have no counterpart in English. It is an unvoiced *Velar*. In pronouncing the velars, the base of the tongue is pulled backwards so as to play against the back of the windpipe. In the case of the letter *Ḥeth*, a complete contact is not made, and in that sense it is akin to the letter *Waw*. It is difficult to describe the sound of *Ḥeth* to those who have never heard it, but it comes close to a stage whisper. Europeans usually pronounce this letter like a Spanish *j* or like the *ch* in *loch*. In transliterations we shall represent its sound by a dotted *H*, thus: *Ḥ*.

ט *Teth* also has no English equivalent. It is an unvoiced dental velar. In other words, the tongue is placed in the dental position as described in our discussion of the letter *Daleth*, while at the same time the base of the tongue is placed in the same position as in the formation of the letter *Ḥeth*. Although Europeans usually do not distinguish this letter from the letter *T*, we transliterate it as *Ṭ*.

י *Yud* is normally pronounced as the English letter *Y* in *yes*; but as we shall see later, it is also occasionally pronounced like the *Y* in *puny*.

כ / ך *Kaf*, like the English letter *K*, is an unvoiced palatal. It, too, suffers from the problems mentioned in our discussion of the letter *Beth*, and its alternative form, written כ, is sounded similarly to the *ch* in the Scottish word *loch*; in transliteration we shall represent it as *Kh*. Note that when *Kaf* appears at the end of a word, it is written in a "final" form as ך. The letters *Mem, Nun, Pe*, and *Ṣaddi* similarly have final forms, as we shall see.

ל *Lammed* is pronounced much like the English letter *L*, except that the tip of the tongue is placed on the dental ridge, as indicated in our discussion of the letter *Daleth*. It differs from the *Daleth* only in that when sounding it, the seal is imperfect, allowing the air to flow around the sides of the tongue.

מ/ם *Mem*. Pronounced like the English letter *M* with the nasal cavity open, the mouth closed by the lips, and the air stream allowed to fill the whole oral cavity. Note the final form ם.

נ/ן *Nun*, pronounced like the English letter *N*, is very similar to the letter *M*, but with the tongue placed in the dental position. Note the final form ן.

ס *Samekh*. The original sound of this letter is not known precisely, but it was certainly some kind of unvoiced sibilant. Today it is pronounced as we pronounce the letter *S*, which is the equivalent of another letter, ש, to be discussed shortly. Since shards from rather early times have been found in which spelling errors occur involving ס and ש, it seems clear that the difference in their sounds was beginning to be lost a long time ago. It remains today only in a few isolated communities.

ע *Ayin* is a voiced velar. Again, this technical term is probably not very useful to the reader, who will be forced to wait for an opportunity to hear a skilled speaker. In European pronunciation, no distinction is made between the *Aleph* and the *Ayin*.

פ/ף *Pe* is an unvoiced bilabial, identical to the English letter *P*, and again requires an alternative, as did the letter *Beth*. Its alternative form is written פ and pronounced like the English letter *F*; we shall transliterate it as *Ph*. Note the final form ף.

צ/ץ *Ṣaddi* is an unvoiced velar sibilant. In other words, with the base of the tongue placed in the ח position, one pronounces the letter *S*. Europeans sometimes pronounce the letter as the English *Ts*; we shall transliterate it as *Ṣ*. Note the final form ץ.

ק *Quph* is a sharp exploded velar similar to the letter *Kaf*, but with contact made between the base of the tongue and the back of the windpipe. As in the case of ס, no need was felt for an alternative form of the sort associated with the letter *Kaf*. Europeans usually do not distinguish in sound between *Quph* and *Kaf*. We shall transliterate ק as *Q*.

		Labial	Laryngeal	Palatal	Dental	Sibilant
Plosive	voiced	ב		ג	ד	
			א			
	unvoiced	פ		כ	ת	
Fricative	voiced	ב		ג	ד	
	unvoiced	פ		ך כ	ת	
Nasal		ם מ			ן נ	
Velar	voiced	ע				
	unvoiced	ח		ק	ט	ץ צ
Open	voiced	ה	ו	י	ר	ז
	unvoiced					ס שׂ
Spread	voiced				ל	
	unvoiced					שׁ

Figure 3.1

ר *Raysh* is similar to the English letter *R*, but again the tip of the tongue is placed on the ridge between the teeth and the palate. It differs from the *Lammed* only in that the tip of the tongue is allowed to vibrate. By tradition, it is trilled three times.

שׁ *Shin* is an unvoiced sibilant similar to the English *Sh*. It differs from *S* in that the air stream is allowed to fan out rather than being directed in a small stream by a curved tongue.

שׂ *Sin* is the precise equivalent of the English *S*. It is interesting to note that while the inventor of the alphabet felt no need to distinguish between שׂ and שׁ (the dots were a later addition), the originator did feel it necessary to distinguish between שׂ and ס.

ת *Taw* is sounded similarly to the English letter *T*, but again the tongue is placed in the dental position. As the reader may already have guessed, its alternative form, ת, is pronounced like *th* in the word *thrice*.

Clearly, the letters almost ask to be ordered. Many of them can be related to others in various ways. However, all such orderings turn out to have two grave defects. First, they are all too messy; second, the authors always cheat, since spoken sounds never correspond precisely to one another. However, the hint of order in the language is great and no author can resist temptation. The table above (Figure 3.1) is somewhat more orderly than most and cheats to about the same degree. In this arrangement each letter is considered to belong to two families of sound, vertical position indicating its mode of articulation, horizontal position indicating the place of its articulation.

4. The Vocalic Modes

Semitic words, and even the syllables that compose them, are a much more formal affair than anything known in the Indo-European languages. In English we adopt foreign words readily and it is no time at all before they sound as American as the hot dog. Occasionally a phrase like *laissez faire* will preserve its foreign flavor, but such is not the general case. The very opposite is true in the Semitic languages. Unless a word has the proper form, it retains its foreign character for thousands of years. On the other hand, the modern Hebrew word *le-tel-pain*, meaning *to telephone*, immediately sounded as if it could have been found in the Bible, since it has all the formal requirements of a Hebrew word.

While the law that regulates the form of the syllable is very simple, its application is somewhat complicated. Dividing a Hebrew word into its syllables is more an art than a science and, as in the case of the art of medicine, even under the most skilled hand the patient sometimes dies. The present chapter should give the reader some experience in learning that skill.

No satisfactory understanding of syllabification in the Hebrew language is possible without a fundamental grasp of the situation as it existed in the proto-Semitic language. In those early times there were only two kinds of syllables. A syllable could consist either of two consonants joined together in what we shall call the short vocalic mode (example: בַּל) or it consisted of a single consonant pronounced in the long vocalic mode (example: בָּ). The first case is called a *closed* syllable because the second consonant closed off the vocalic flow. The second case is called an *open* syllable because it ended with an inherently continuous vocalic sound. Our whole discussion will, of course, be somewhat anachronistic, since proto-Semitic was never a written language. But this device will enable us to get a clearer picture of the Hebrew language as it existed in Biblical times.

Originally there were three types of vocalic modes, qualitatively speaking: *A*, as in the word *father*; *I*, as in the word *ink*; and *U*, pronounced like the *oo* sound in *moon*. Though for the sake of brevity we shall continue to use the word *vowel*, the reader must constantly remember that the Semitic languages contain no vowels as entities in themselves, and that it would be better to speak of the three vocalic modes in which a letter such as בּ might be pronounced. From a quantitative point of view, there were two or perhaps three lengths of vocalic modes. We shall begin by considering the first two lengths and then raise the difficulties concerning the third.

In spite of the even greater anachronism involved, we shall introduce the fifth-century marks that distinguish the modes of pronunciation. The vocalic modes that will interest us first are:

	I	*A*	*U*
short mode:	בִ	בַ	בֻ
long mode:	בִ	בָ	בֻ

The marks designating the *I*, *A*, and *U* modes have the following names:[1]

	I	*A*	*U*
short mode:	חִרֶק (ḥireq)	פָּתַּח (pataḥ)	קֻבֵּץ (qubuṣ)
long mode:	חִרֶק (ḥireq)	קָמָץ (qamaṣ)	קֻבֵּץ (qubuṣ)

Their names derive from the following root meanings:

חרק : to scratch   קבץ : to gather

קמץ : to close   פתח : to open

Sometimes no vowel is required. When this is the case, a sign called the *shewa* is placed under the letter (example: בְ) as a kind of place-holder. The word *shewa* itself means *empty* or *vain*. We shall see other instances in which the Masoretes used signs which, though they had no value in themselves, made it clear that no other sign had accidentally fallen out of the text. For instance, it sometimes happens that a letter which, for one reason or another, one might have expected to have a dagesh, in fact has none. In such cases the Masoretes put a line, called a *rapha*, over the letter (for example: בֿ) to signify that the dagesh had been left out intentionally.

---

1. *I*, *A*, and *U* were the only vocalic modes in proto-Semitic; two additional modes developed later.

In proto-Semitic all syllables had, as it were, the same "weight." A closed syllable, consisting of two letters, would be sounded in a short mode; while an open syllable, consisting of a single letter, would be pronounced in the long mode.

Some examples may help. The word for *man* was אָדָם. Thus, we have a word with three open syllables, אָ-דָ-ם each of which, therefore, was pronounced in the long mode. The word for *dog*, on the other hand (כַּלְבָּ) was a two-syllable word, כַּלְ-בָּ. The first syllable, being closed, was pronounced in the short mode, but the last syllable, since it was open, was pronounced in the long mode.

The reader will also note that the ד in the word אָדָם has no dagesh because it follows an open syllable—or, alternatively, because it is led into from a vocalic sound. On the other hand, the כ in the word כַּלְבָּ receives a dagesh because it is a beginning, whereas the ב receives a dagesh because the preceding syllable is closed off by the ל; in that sense the ב also marks a new beginning.

As we shall see, Biblical Hebrew generally accents the last syllable, called the *ultima*. However, the earliest form of the Semitic languages, which we are now considering, accented the next to the last syllable, called the *penult*. Thus we have such words as אָ-דָ-ם and כַּלְ-בָּ. (An underline here marks the accented syllable.)

Some scholars believe that there was an even earlier stage in which the accent fell upon the *antepenult*, that is, one syllable before the *penult*. However, since no trace of this stage has left its mark on the Hebrew language, the existence of such a stage would be a mere historical fact of no present interest to us. If, on the other hand, we were to turn from Hebrew to the general subject of comparative grammar of the Semitic languages, such a long-dead historical fact might suddenly come to life again for us.

Exercise: Read and give an account of the syllables and vocalic modes:

1. בָּרַךְ דָּוִד מִן נָוָת   2. אָבַד בָּקַשׁ נַפְשִׁי
3. יָשַׁבְתָּ עִם הֶן מֶלֶךְ   4. זָבַח הֶן יָמִים
5. הוּא גָּנַב

In the last chapter we looked at one kind of dagesh, the small dot that distinguishes the בּ from ב to mark the beginning of a new flow of breath. The same mark, however, is often used for a totally different purpose.

There is disagreement among scholars concerning the nature of this second kind of dagesh. Some call it a *doubling* dagesh, while others call it a *strengthening* dagesh. As is so often the case, this disagreement has arisen because the world often falls between the terms of our technical jargon, and the full understanding of the problem is often identical to its solution.

In the last the exercise we had the word גָּנַב. There existed, however, another word which could have been written גַּנְנַב but was in fact written גַּנָּב. It had three syllables, גַּ-נָּ-ב, which leads some scholars to refer to the נ as a double letter. Those who object to this terminology fear that it may lead to a slight pause between the two נ's. The double letter should be made as one continuous sound. You can get a better feeling for making this sound by practicing with the letter *P*. In English there is the implosive *P*, such as we have in the word *lamp*, as well as the explosive *P*, such as we have in the word *post*. You will then pretty much have the sound under control by pronouncing the word *lamppost* as a single word. The effect is just about the same as some readers may already be familiar with in the Italian word *bella*.

Perhaps you may have noted that at this stage in pre-Biblical Hebrew, most of the words end in a vocalic mode. In many instances these modes determined the *case* of the word. דָּוִד was simply a noun—the name of a young man who became king in Israel, David. It primarily named the actor, or what we today would call *the nominative case*. On the other hand, דָוִד was not a name, but rather a cross between what we call a *noun* and what we call a *preposition*. דָוִד meant *to David* and as such was often used where we would use a *direct object*, or an adverb. דָוִד saw me, but I saw דָוִד—that is, *I saw David* or *I saw Davidwards*. In the same vein, דָוִד meant *from David*. Little is left of this final vowel except for an occasional word like יְרוּשָׁלַיְמָה meaning *Jerusalem-wards*, but as we shall see, its effect is great.

At some point after proto-Semitic began to differentiate itself into its several branches, Hebrew and the family to which it belonged dropped the vocalic mode of its final sound. Thus, אָדָם became אָדָם and שֻׁלְחָן became שֻׁלְחָן. In a later chapter we shall consider the genesis of the prepositions, but for the moment let it suffice to say that once the speakers began to frame prepositions, they may no longer have felt any need for the final vocalic mode.

When the final vowel was dropped, however, no other alterations were made. As a consequence, two major changes in the language took place. In most cases the accent, while it still fell on the same letter, now fell on the last syllable, the ultima. Therefore the final syllable, in spite of being closed, continued to be pronounced in the long mode; for example, אָ-דָ-ם became אָדָם.

On the other hand, consider the word כַּלְבֻּ. When the final vowel was dropped, only the form כַּלְב remained, and so it is pronounced today in modern spoken Arabic, partly because speakers of Arabic do not need or have the sound ב, and even Classical Arabic finds no difficulty in ending a syllable with the sound ב. But to a Hebrew-speaking tongue such a syllable was simply unpronounceable.

Through usage, two ways of handling the problem arose. Normally that strange doubly-closed syllable pronounced in the short mode, כַּלְב, was broken up into two syllables, each of which is pronounced in a new and even shorter mode. This mode is like the *e* in the word *bed*. The word came to be pronounced *ke-lev*, and was written כֶּלֶב. The name of the new vocalic sign is *segol*. This time too the accent remained on the same syllable, but it is now an open syllable pronounced in a very short mode, כֶּ-לֶב. However, this pattern is not always followed. The word נַעַר became נַעַר and פַּתְחַ became פֶּתַח because both ע and ח prefer the *A* mode. But note that at this stage the *segol* is not yet part of a general system.

Sometimes this solution was felt not to work. Take the word צֶבַע, meaning *finger*. It would have become צֶבַע; but the speakers felt that the syllable צֶ was too weak for such a word, and so they developed the form אֶצְבָּע. We can hear the difference ourselves by comparing the *e* in the word *edit* with the *e* in *desk*. The *e* in *edit* is just a mite stronger than the *e* in *desk*. Here in אֶצְבָּע the א has almost become only a means of putting the *e*-sound before the ṣ-sound. That means that this segol has become something more than just a mode.

As an interesting means of comparing Formal Grammar to Intentional Grammar, it should be pointed out that from the point of view of Formal Grammar, most of what has been said in this chapter could have been given in the form of four simple laws:

1. An <u>open unaccented syllable</u> takes a long vowel: דָּבָר
2. A <u>closed accented syllable</u> takes a long vowel: דָּבָר
3. An <u>open accented syllable</u> takes a short vowel: כֶּלֶב
4. An <u>closed unaccented syllable</u> takes a short vowel: כֶּלֶב

These laws can be summarized in the following chart:

	OPEN	CLOSED
ACCENTED	short	long
UNACCENTED	long	short

From the formalistic point of view there is no past; these laws apply without any mention of a dropped final vowel. We ask, however, which way best leads to human intelligibility?

Earlier we made mention of a third kind of vocalic mode. The difficulties involved can be seen by looking at the word for *city street*, which appears in ancient Hebrew manuscripts as שוק but appears in ancient Phoenician manuscripts in the form שק.

Originally, the word probably had the form שָׁוְק. It seems clear that the Phoenician scribe was hearing the consonant ו as if it had somehow become the vocalic mode of the שׁ, since ו was pronounced with the sound of our W. If the Phoenician scribe had had vocalic mode signs at his disposal, he would have written שׁק.

But what of the Hebrew scribe who did not yet have vocalic mode signs? Was he still hearing the ו as a consonant and writing it as such, to yield שָׁוְק? Or was he too beginning to hear it as some kind of a vowel, שׁוק? Perhaps there was no need to ask the question until the dropping of the final vocalic mode. Once that had occurred, שוק had to become a one-syllable word, and consequently ו implicitly became what we shall call a *consonantal vowel*, since at this point the ו can no longer be regarded as a simple consonant; nor, on the other hand, can it be viewed as the mere mode in which the שׁ is pronounced; rather it is on its way to having a sound of its own—as does a true vowel. (For a corresponding English example, what shall we say of the *w* in the word *bow*?) Still, the vocalic ו cannot stand on its own as a vowel except when it is forced to substitute for the consonant ‍ו for euphonic reasons. In later times the vocalic ו would be distinguished by a dot: וֹ. For very similar reasons, there is a vocalic *yud* (יִ), and there probably was even a vocalic *aleph* (אַ) in pre-Biblical Hebrew.

We can now expand the chart on page 26 above to include the consonantal vowels. In the next chapter we will discuss a vocalic shift that led to a broader vocalic system.

	I	*A*	*U*
short mode:	בִ	בַ	בֻ
long mode:	בֵ	בָ	בֹ
consonantal vowel:	בִי	בָא	בוּ

In the Biblical text the distinction between the long mode and the consonantal vowels is not always maintained. Quite often an author will write a word with a long vowel and within a few verses repeat the word using the consonantal vowel. In general, however, there is a tendency to avoid a multiplicity of consonantal vowels in the same word.

A few modern scholars have even raised some doubts as to whether any meaningful distinction can be made between the two. Some even dispute the distinction between the *long* and the *short* mode altogether. Perhaps the most thoughtful of these authors is Alexander Sperber, whose book *Hebrew Grammar, A New Approach* is written with true humanity and deep concern. While the conclusions of that book are very different from my own, the book should be read by any serious student.

5. What is a Syllable?

In addition to the dropping of the final vowel (and, so for as I can see, nearly though not totally independent of it), there were a number of shifts in vocalic mode that occurred over time, and which may be seen as a whole in the following chart:

	I	E	A	O	U
Short Mode	בִּ→	בֶּ	בַּ	בָּ	בֻּ
Long Mode	בִּ→	בֵּ	בָּ	בֹּ	בָּ←
Consonantal Vowel	בִּי	בֵּי	בָּא→	בּוֹ	בּוּ

1. The consonantal vowel A (אָ) came to be pronounced as the *ou* in the word *nought*, though for the sense of symmetry, we shall call it the *O* mode. It was symbolized at first as בּו, but after the invention of the dot notation it became בּוֹ. Often, however, the ו was deleted, and the scribes would simply write בֹּ. It appears that the shift from consonantal A to consonantal O must have taken place before the invention of writing; at any rate, the בָּא form no longer exists as a consonantal vowel in Biblical Hebrew.

2. The consonantal I (יִ) was retained, but both the long and short I became E, as indicated in the chart. (As we shall see, the I mode will return, but from a different source.) The E vowel, as we saw, has a short form, called a segol. The vocalic shift from I to E then gave rise to a long E, בֵּ, called צֵרֵה (ṣere). Thus חֵנ became חֵן, but בֵּנ became בֵּן. The צֵרֵה is pronounced like the Greek letter η or like the *é*'s in the French word *été*. In English the sound never appears by itself, but it does occur as the first half of the diphthong in the word *plate*.[1]

3. In most cases the long U became a consonantal O. Thus כֵּל became כּוֹל.

4. Ultimately the E and O vocalic modes developed the full range of lengths as indicated in the charts. From this point on,

---

1. Or as the word *plate* itself is pronounced in Jamaica.

however, there is a fundamental disagreement within the tradition. Everyone agrees that the consonantal *A* (בָּא) became a consonantal *O* (בוֹ, pronounced like the *ou* in *nought*), while the short *A* (בַּ) retained its *A* quality. However, in most of the Oriental communities the long *A* (בָּ) also retained its status as a long *A*, while in the communities of Northern Europe its sound, along with that of the consonantal *A*, shifted to *O*.

The names of these vocalic signs are as follows:

	I	*E*	*A*	*O*	*U*
Short Mode	חִרֶק	סֶגֹל	פָּתֶח	קָמֶץ Small	קֻבֶּץ
Long Mode	חִרֶק	צֵרֶה	קָמֶץ Great	חֹלֶם	קֻבֶּץ
Consonantal Vowel	חִרֶק	צֵרֶה Full		חֹלֶם Full	שֻׁרֶק

Another major change that took place involves a new kind of syllable that tends to show up near the beginning of long words. For instance, consider the word דָּבָר which, in Biblical Hebrew, became דָּבָר. The masculine plural ending in Hebrew, which we must discuss in greater detail at another place, is ־ים . Therefore one would expect the plural to be דָּבָרִים. But because of a tendency to lighten the beginning of long words a change took place. In Hebrew, the word is written דְּבָרִים. The first letter came to be pronounced *d'*, where the little ‘ is pronounced *uh,* or somewhat like the *u* in *umbrella.* As the reader has no doubt noticed, the symbol under the ד is identical to the shewa; the shewa that we already know is called a resting shewa; this one is called a moving shewa for reasons we are about to explain.

At this point, syllabification becomes somewhat difficult. To the western ear, דְּבָרִים would seem to be a three-syllable word, דְּ-בָ-רִים; but it might be more in the spirit of the Semitic languages to call דְּבָ a new kind of syllable, rather than allowing the sound דְּ the status of a syllable in its own right.

The two shewa modes may be distinguished from one another by the fact that the moving shewa comes at the beginning of a syllable, while the resting shewa must always come at the end of a syllable.

The following rules of thumb, which are the direct consequences of what has been said, will be helpful in distinguishing the moving shewa mode from the resting shewa mode:

1. A shewa at the beginning of a word is a moving shewa (example: דְּבָרִים).

2. If two shewas appear in succession, the first must be resting, and the second moving (example: חַסְדְּךָ).

3. If a shewa follows a long mode or a consonantal vowel, it is moving (e.g., כָּתְבוּ).

4. If a shewa accompanies a consonant with a dagesh, the situation is almost as if there were two shewas, the second of which is moving (example: דִּבְּרוּ).

Since these rules of thumb are merely derivative, they should be understood rather than memorized.

There yet remains some difficulty in connection with the third rule. It arises from the fact that the mark for the short *O* is indistinguishable in shape from that for the long *A*. In general there is no great problem. If the syllable is open it is a long *A*, as in כָּ; if closed, a short *O*, as in כָּת. But consider the word כָּתְבוּ. How can one know in this case whether the קָמָץ is a long *A* or a short *O*? In other words, is the first syllable כָּ, in the long *A* mode, or is it כָּת, in the short *O* mode? In this particular case either an application of the rule or a simple good feeling for the sounds of the language will give a solution to our problem. If the shewa were resting the word would have to be spelled כָּת-בּוּ, with a dagesh in the בּ; that is not what we have. If, on the other hand, the shewa is moving, the spelling must be כָּ-תְבוּ, which is in fact the spelling we are given.

I hope working through this example was a bit of fun for the reader, but the same approach does not succeed in all cases. Consider the word אָזְנֶךָ. Is it to be pronounced אָזְ-נֶךָ or אָ-זְנֶךָ? Normally one would just have to ask a knowledgeable speaker. But if we consult the Biblical text, we find words like הֲלְאָה. The little line next to the קָמָץ in the word הֲלְאָה is called a *metheg*, and it is often used to mark the end of a syllable when things might otherwise be unclear. Since אָזְנֶךָ appears without a metheg, while הֲלְאָה has one, we may infer that we are to pronounce אָזְ-נֶךָ in the one case, but הָ-לְאָה in the other.

As things stand at this point, the consonantal *A* along with both the short and long *I* have all disappeared from the language. However, the *I* sound reappeared as a consequence of the tendency to lighten the beginning of long words, discussed in the last chapter. For instance, according to that law, the word מַכְתָּב would have become מְכְתָּב. As we can see, the first syllable (מְכְ) contains two shewas, the first moving, the second resting. It was only natural, given their sense of what a syllable was, that speakers tended to give a bit more body to such a syllable. Thus, the word became מִכְתָּב.

Exactly the same principle, though in a somewhat hidden form, can be seen at work in the word לִמֵּד. Bearing in mind that the dagesh really implies an original form לַמְמֵד, it would follow that the form would have gone to לְמֵּד. But in fact, under the euphonic influence of the חִרֶק, the word went to לִמֵּד.

Occasionally difficulties arise in giving a particular form to a particular root. This happens when the form requires a shewa on one of the letters א, ה, ח, ע, or ר, since these sounds have insufficient character in themselves to be clearly audible in the shewa mode. The problem is especially critical with א and ע. In these cases, the shewa needs a little help, and three new vocalic modes almost naturally came to be. They are:

אֲ	in the *A* mode, called	פַּתָח חַטֶף
אֳ	in the *O* mode, called	קָמֶץ חַטֶף
אֱ	in the *E* mode, called	סֶגוֹל חַטֶף

where the word חַטֶף (hatuph) means *to be snatched away*.

In the case of a resting shewa the mode of the חַטֶף generally agrees with the mode of the syllable in which the shewa occurs. For example, we find צָהֳרִים instead of צָהְרִים; the צָהֳ is considered to be one syllable with a bit of a bounce to it. However, here again ע and ח seem to prefer the *A* mode to the *E* mode. In the case of a moving shewa, the חַטֶף is often used to give body to a guttural, as in the word שָׁחֲטוּ. Although the *A* mode is normally preferred, euphony has a large part to play. Non-gutturals can also appear as hatuphim for a variety of euphonic reasons.

Hatuphim can strengthen and preserve the doubleness of a shewa:

הְלֲלוּ ← הַלְלוּ

Ḥatuphim can keep a sibilant firmly in its own syllable:

וּ-שְׁמָע,

or keep a velar strong:

הוּטְלוּ.

And they do many other things.

The development of the moving shewa gave rise to an alternative solution to the problem raised by the word כַּלְבּ. As we saw in Chapter 4, this word became כֶּלֶב, while a word like זַרְע became אֶזְרַע. The moving shewa allowed for different solutions; for example, the word דְּבַשׁ became דְּבָשׁ.

Exercise: Read I Samuel Chapter 20, verses 1–6 (page 175 below). Try to account for the vocalic mode of each syllable, bearing in mind what has been said about the dropping of the final letter as well as the significance of the dagesh. Since we have not yet learned all the tricks of the trade, if you can account for three-quarters of them, you will be doing quite well.

One day during my first year of trying to learn some Hebrew, I came across the word בָּמָה. It is in fact a rather common word, the one King James' men usually translated "high place." It had the perfect form for a Hebrew word, and yet it rang foreign to my ear and would hardly come off my tongue, though I had no idea why. The rest of this chapter is meant to bring some insight into what my ear was picking up.

Semitic words are no less definite in their forms than the syllables of which they are composed. Most, if not all, are based on roots made up of three consonants. These roots have been forged into words in two different ways: first, by specifying the vocalic mode of each letter of the root, and second, by adding other letters. Most of our work will consist of trying to understand the genesis of the grammatical forms. Before doing so, however, let us consider the roots themselves.

The general law for the composition of roots is *variety*. There is a general tendency to avoid repetition in sound, although under certain circumstances, repetition is often played with quite artfully. We can summarize the various cases with these rules:

1. No root is composed of three identical letters.

2. The first two letters of a root are rarely identical.

3. The first and last letters of a root are rarely identical.[2]

4. Finally, the second and third letters of a root are often identical, and such roots interplay with similar roots having ו as the middle letter.

For the sake of ease, we have introduced two signs:

פ⟵#‒מ means that if מ appears in a root, פ cannot follow it.[3]

ב⟵#⟶פ means that פ and ב may not occur in the same root. The restricted cases are charted here.

Laryngeal–Laryngeal:

ה⟵#⟶ח   ה⟵#⟶ע   ח⟵#⟶ע   א⟵#⟶ע

Bilabial–Bilabial:

מ⟵#⟶ב (exception: במה)   מ‒#⟶פ   ב⟵#⟶פ

Palatal–Palatal:

ק⟵#⟶כ   ק⟵#⟶ג   כ⟵#⟶ג

Dental–Dental:

ד‒#⟶ט(exception: אטד)   ת⟵#⟶ד   ט⟵#⟶ת

Sibilant–Sibilant:

ש⟵#⟶ז   ס⟵#⟶צ   ס⟵#⟶ז

ש⟵#‒ס   ש⟵#⟶צ   צ⟵#⟶ז

ש⟵#‒ס   צ⟵#⟶ש

Dental–Palatal:

כ‒#⟶ט   ג⟵#⟶ט

Sibilant–Palatal:

כ⟵#⟶צ   ג⟵#‒צ   ג⟵#⟶ז

---

2. To this third rule there is a major exception. There exists a large family of roots whose middle root letter is either ו or י and whose first and third root letters are identical; in these cases, the middle letter becomes vocalic, as in סוס, תות, and others. Moreover, we find four other curious cases: שרש, שמש, שלש, and סרס. It is interesting to note that in each of these four, the first and third root letters are sibilants, while on the other hand ל and ר are phonetically akin.

3. "Follow" here means in the direction of Hebrew writing, right to left.

Dental–Sibilant:

ת–#←ז   ט→#←ז   ד–#←ז

ת–#←ס (exception: תמס)   ט→#←ס   ד–#←ס

ת–#←צ (exception: נתץ)   ט→#←צ   ד–#←צ

ת–#←שׁ (exception: תרש)   ט–#←שׁ   ד–#←שׁ

There are no restrictions on the following cases:

Laryngeal–Bilabial

Laryngeal–Palatal

Laryngeal–Sibilant

Bilabial–Palatal

Bilabial–Dental

Many scholars have argued that at an earlier stage, the Semitic languages were based on two-letter rather than three-letter roots. Their arguments seem to me rather shaky from a historical point of view, and they add little to our understanding of the formation of the language. But they do point to another, rather important, aspect of the language.

Many words in Hebrew are both close in meaning and close in sound. Often their roots do not exist in isolation but tend to come in clusters. Now if the hypothesis of two-letter roots were true, all the members of each cluster would have two letters in common and would differ only in the third letter. This, however, is far from being the case. For example, consider the words זבל and סבל. Both words mean *to bear*, but we have no evidence that there was ever a root בל. The following discussion is an attempt to convey something of the character of the root clusters.

Some clusters are very large, but by examining them carefully one can get a feeling for the way in which the language may have developed—one letter changing here, another changing there. As in the case of זבל and סבל, the reader must constantly be thinking of the sounds of the letters in order to follow the growth of the roots.

Interestingly enough, a cluster often consists of two or more words that sound alike or nearly alike, but which are opposite in meaning. For instance, סכל means *to be stupid* and שׂכל means *to be wise*. One might be tempted to say that we recognized the coin

before we recognized either of its faces, but the reader will have
to think each case through on its own merits.

SOME ROOT CLUSTERS:

I

1. זבח to sacrifice   2. סבח to cook

II

1. סכל to be stupid   2. שכל to be wise

III

1. זבל to bear   2. סבל to bear

IV

1. טבל to dip   2. טבע to sink or imprint

V

1. נהר river   2. נחל stream

VI

1. צאק to cry out   3. צחק to laugh
2. צעק to yell   4. שׂחק to cry out

VII

1. אוף to hasten   3. עוף to fly
2. דוף to leap

VIII

1. נצב to be well established 3. ישׁב to dwell or sit
2. יצב to be firm or hold one's 4. שׁכב to recline
   ground

IX

1. נגד to be in front of   4. נגשׁ to draw near
2. נגע to touch   5. נשׂג to reach
3. נגף to strike

X

1. ארג to weave
2. ארז to make firm with ropes

3. אזר to gird oneself

3a. אחז to grasp

4. אסר to bind

4a. אחר to bind or enchant

5. אסף to gather or collect

XI

1. גזה to cut

2. גזז to shear

2a. גזר to shear, decide, cut in pieces, or to slaughter

2b. גז to cut, hence the name of a caterpillar

3. גזל to cut, tear, steal

4. גזע to saw

5. גרז to exterminate

6. גרש to grind

7. גרס to crush or bruise

XII

1. לחם to fight hand-to-hand

4. לכד to catch

2. לחץ to squeeze, press, or vex

5. לקח to take

3. לחת to gather, pick, glean

6. לקש to snatch (take in haste)

XIII

1. הוה to desire

2. אוה to desire or long for

3. אבה to be willing, to consent

4. אהב to love

4a. חבב to burn or to love

4b. חבק to embrace

5. אוב to be together

6. איב to be hostile toward

As you see, some clusters can be quite large, and there are undoubtedly many other roots which have gone unnoticed in our chart. I have tried to arrange the roots in such a way as to suggest the way in which the language developed by substituting sound for sound. Needless to say, there is no claim of having rediscovered the precise paths that were taken; the lists present an appearance of a linear development, but historically it was surely a massive entanglement. The following diagram summarizes the kinds of changes that took place:

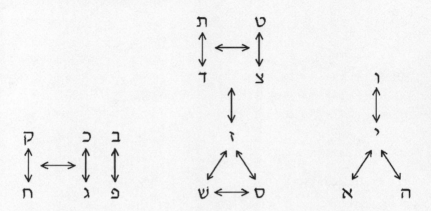

Additionally, one or more of the root letters of the members of a cluster may sometimes be dropped or replaced by a quasi-silent letter. Such a cluster is the following.

XIV.

1. אחד one
2. אגד to bind
3. גוד to attack
4. גדד to gather together against
5. גדע to cut off or mutilate
6. גת winepress
7. כרת to cut off or divorce
8. כתב to inscribe or write
9. קתב to cut off
10. קתף to pluck
11. קצב to butcher
12. קצח to break off
13. קצה end or border
14. קצע to break off
15. קצף to trim a beard
16. קצר to reap, to be short
17. קוץ a thorn
18. קץ end
19. חצב to hew
20. חצי half
21. חקר to explore, dig
22. חקה to carve
23. חקק to inscribe or give laws
24. דקק to beat thin
25. דפק to rap on a door
26. דוך to pound (in a mortar)
27. דכח to crush (for nuts)
28. דכא to crush

6. What is a Person?

The Hebrew pronoun provides the basis of the formal aspect of the language and it is there that we must start.

As in most languages, Hebrew personal pronouns are an etymological nightmare. They do, however, play a considerable role in the formal structure of the language and therefore deserve our most careful attention. This inquiry will also give us some insight into the growth of the language and the shifts in its sounds.

We shall begin by comparing the personal pronouns in Hebrew with those of Arabic on the one hand and Akkadian on the other (Table 6.1). The reader should be warned that while the transliteration of Arabic into Hebrew characters is relatively simple (since the Arabic alphabet is also a direct descendent of the Phoenician), the Akkadian transliteration is not quite so straightforward. Akkadian, you will recall, was written in a syllabary adapted from Sumerian cuneiform. It contains no glottal stop, but words can begin with the vocalic-like sounds. This means that in our transliterations of Akkadian, aleph (א) will be used only as an occasion for using a vowel sign.

It should be noted that both Akkadian and Arabic still retain the consonantal long *A* sound, symbolized as א, which in Hebrew has become a long *O*.

If we start with the gross phenomena, we can note that the plurals differ from the singulars by the addition of a מ or נ. Both these letters are commonly used in the formation of plurals of nouns as well as verbs in most of the Semitic languages, and they will be discussed in another place.

The first thing to strike one in Table 6.1 is the similarity among the languages. This similarity is, in fact, even greater than might appear at first glance. In Hebrew the letter נ is very weak and unstable. Thus when נ is accompanied by a resting shewa it becomes assimilated to the following letter. For example, instead of אַנְתָּה one has אַתָּה, where the נ is hidden in the dagesh. Note that the assimilated נ was felt so strongly that a dagesh even appears in the second-person feminine in a manner that breaks every rule of syllabification, in that תְּ has now almost become a full syllable in its own right.

	Arabic	*Hebrew*	*Akkadian*
Singular			
3rd per. masc.	הֻו	הוּא	שׂוּ
3rd per. fem.	הִי	הִיא	שׂי
2nd per. masc.	אַנְתַ	אַתָּה	אַתָּא
2nd per. fem.	אַנְתִ	אַתְּ	אַתִּי
1st per. c.	אָנָא	אָנֹכִי \ אֲנִי	אָנָאכֻ
Plural			
3rd per. masc.	הֻמֻו	הֵם	שׂנֻ
3rd per. fem.	הֻנַ	הֵנָה \ הֵן	שׂנַ
2nd per. masc.	אַתֻמֻו	אַתֶּם	אַתֻ
2nd per. fem.	אַנְתֻנָּאא	תֵּנָה \ אַתֵּן	אַתֻנַ
1st per. c.	נַחֻ	אֲנַחְנוּ \ אָנוּ	נֻ

Table 6.1. Semitic Pronouns

In Hebrew the letter ת is also considered weak. Its weakness lies in the fact that it tends to drop out when it is the feminine ending and stands as the final letter of the word.

From what we have seen so far, it appears that the root of the first person is אָנֹך \ אנח and that of the second person, אנת. That may be the case, and yet if they are truly two independent roots, one is left to wonder why they should just happen have the first two root letters אנ in common, and differ only in the third. The problem will become even more confusing when we develop the verb.

We might gain insight from another Semitic language. In Ethiopian the first person singular of the verb based on the root ילד \ ולד is וָלַדְכֻ as one might have expected; but in Hebrew one finds יָלַדְתִּי, and most of the other Semitic languages agree in using the ת as the subjective formative for both the first and the second persons. On the other hand, in several other forms the כ will show up in the second person. One is then led to suspect either that אנת and אנכ are merely alternative forms of the same

root or, what is more likely, that the common root is אנת and the
כ has crept in from a כה or כא, meaning *this* or *here*. During the
course of the next few chapters, as we look at the verbs, we will see
again that the formations of the first- and second-person forms
are similar and quite distinct from the third-person form.

The Hebrew root אנת also appears in the preposition אֶת,
which means *together with, in communion with*, or *beside* and which
usually implies peaceful togetherness. People often sign covenants
with (אֶת) each other; and God tells Moses, "There is a place with
(אֶת) me." When endings are added to it, the ת always has a
dagesh. For example, the word אִתִּי, *with me*, implies an earlier
form אנתי, or again that the original root was אנת.

These reflections and discoveries would seem to suggest that
the first and second persons were of common origin, an origin
based on the notion of togetherness, and that only later was *I*
distinguished from *you*.

Among the Semitic languages there is apparently greater
diversity in the third-person personal pronouns than in the
second-person personal pronouns. Hebrew and Arabic, however,
are somewhat closer than would appear at first. The Arabic
suggests that the old Hebraic form might have contained a vocalic
א which was retained in the Hebrew script but not in the Arabic.
The fact that most Hebrew words have at least three letters might
have encouraged such a retention.

The root הוא is part of a cluster that include root הוה or היה,
meaning *to be* or *to become*. Earlier we mentioned a difference
between the first- and second-person verbal endings on the one
hand, and the third-person endings on the other. The most
fundamental difference is that the third person requires no verbal
ending at all: כָּתַב means *he wrote*, just as כָּתַבְתִּי means *I wrote*. The
first person requires a formative ending, but the third person
requires nothing more than the bare root itself. This would imply
that to speak means primarily to speak of a thing that is *found
there*—that is, as a third person. From this point of view, *to be*
means *to be a phenomenon*; and in fact Hebrew often predicates
existence by saying such and such *is found* (or, as the context
usually makes clear, *is findable*). To *be*, in other words, is to be a
that. This facet of the world stands in contradistinction to the
Cartesian notion that to *be* is primarily to be a *thinking subject*.

7. On Predication

Although Biblical Hebrew does contain what might be described as the distinction between nouns and verbs, that distinction is somewhat superficial and lacks the fundamental character that it has in most Indo-European languages. Let us begin this chapter, then, by trying to understand a speech in which that distinction is lacking. Consider the following four sentences:

1. דָּוִד אָדָם
2. דָּוִד כָּתַב
3. דָּוִד קָטֹן
4. דָּוִד חָכָם

The first three sentences would normally be translated as:

1. David is a man
2. David writes.
3. David is small.

From a formal point of view, all four Hebrew sentences are structurally identical in that they have the same vocalic pattern. One should also note that none of the sentences contains anything corresponding to the English verb *is*. Merely by placing the words together on the page, or by speaking them successively in time, the writer or speaker has made a declaration for which he must be responsible. The identical form of these sentences might lead us to wonder whether we should not have translated the first sentence *David mans*, or *David is manning*, or perhaps even *David is a manning-thing*. Similarly, דָּוִד כָּתַב might be translated *David is a writer* or *David is a writing-one*. These rather barbaric renderings are an attempt to show the noun- or adjective-like character of the verb and the verb- or adjective-like character of the noun. While the word אָדָם in Biblical Hebrew is undoubtedly a noun, the fact that דָּוִד אָדָם is a perfectly good sentence betrays the verb-like character of its origin.

Our fourth sentence, דָּוִד חָכָם, is perhaps a clearer indication of the problem. It may be translated *David is wise*, *David is a wise man*, or *David is being wise*.

Consider the sentence אָדָם סָכָל, where אָדָם means *man* and סָכָל means *foolish* or *is foolish*. By merely by placing these words together we intend to reflect a togetherness that exists totally apart from our speech. As we know, the sentence might be translated equally well as *a man is a foolish thing*, or *a man acts foolishly*, or even *a manning thing is a fool*. Perhaps, then, rather than "predicating" one idea of another (the title of this chapter) it would be better to speak of "placing ideas together." For the words אָדָם סָכָל need not be construed as a sentence at all; they could be translated simply as *a foolish man*. We could, for instance, say אָדָם סָכָל כָּתַב, *a foolish man writes*. In the English translation we have taken the word *foolish* to be part of the subject and the word *writes* to be the predicate, but pre-Biblical Hebrew may have only intended to indicate the concrete togetherness of the three ideas.

As time went on, people in their speech and in their thoughts must have begun to feel the need for making finer distinctions. Some situations around them were no longer adequately captured by pointing to the togetherness of two or more thoughts in a concrete *this*. Sometimes one idea was more dependent on the other, while the other was seen to be more independent.

For instance, the word שָׂכָר must have meant something like *wages* or *recompense* or *hire*. As we learned in Chapter 4, it then became שָׂכָר. But then people began to put words together. They would say שָׂכַר דָּוִד, meaning *wages of David*. Notice that the two words have almost been treated as a single word: the vocalic mode of the syllable כַר has become short, as if it fell in the middle of a word. Often the law of lightening applies. דָּבָר means *word*, but *the word of David* is דְּבַר דָּוִד. Whether the two words have actually become one, (as happens in German, for example) is a very difficult question and one we are not prepared to face.

The form דְּבַר (as distinguished from דָּבָר) is referred to by western grammarians as the *construct* form. In Hebrew it is called the *leaning* form, which might be a bit more descriptive of its true function, as we shall see. The leaning form is very common and is used where some western languages use the genitive case.

Nevertheless the way in which the words interact is somewhat different. In western languages we would say "word" (nominative) "of David" (genitive). In the Semitic languages things are cut a bit differently; one says "word of" (leaning form) "David" (absolute form). Perhaps, then, the best way to render דְּבַר is "word of ..."; for דְּבַר is not a word that can stand on its own, rather it must "lean" on the word that follows it.

Something like this is also found among the western languages, though we are less aware of it now than in former times. The Greek word for *case* is $\pi\tau\hat{\omega}\sigma\iota\varsigma$, from $\pi\acute{\iota}\pi\tau\omega$, *to fall*. We think of Greek as having five cases, Nominative, Genitive, Dative, Accusative, and Vocative, as if the word *case* meant *a kind* or *an instance* rather than *a falling*—even though the word *case* itself comes from the Latin *cadere,* meaning *to fall.* The first Greek grammarians probably did not think of the Nominative as a case. It was simply the name of the object. The cases or fallings were more like *inclinations to or from,* or *dispositions with respect to,* an object. In that sense, the cases may have had a significance somewhere between what we would call nouns and what we call prepositions. It may even help sometimes to consider adverbs as cases; think, for example, of *townwards* as the accusative "falling" of the word *town.*

Thus far we have spoken only of the masculine gender; we must now speak of the feminine gender. At first it was normally formed by the addition of תְ, though often a connecting vowel was required. Thus the feminine form of the masculine חָדָשׁ was חֲדָשֶׁתְ. When the final vowel was dropped, the ת became silent. But since there was now no written sign for the vocalic mode, the ת could not be simply dropped without losing the distinction between חָדָשׁ and חָדָשׁ. Therefore a vocalic ה was placed at the end of the feminine form, a ghost of the original ת; and the word became חֲדָשָׁה. The softening of the ת, however, did not affect the leaning form, because it was still felt to be somehow in the middle of a word. Thus, the leaning form of the feminine חֲדָשָׁה is חֲדָשַׁת.

As we shall see later, the feminine plural is formed by lengthening the vocalic mode of the root ending. Thus the plural of חֲדָשַׁת became חֲדָשָׂאתְ and hence חֲדָשׁוֹת. Note that in this case too the final ת was not dropped.

	Masc.	Fem.
Singular	חָדָשׁ	חֲדָשָׁה
Plural	חֲדָשִׁים	חֲדָשׁוֹת

When discussing gender, it is sometimes necessary to distinguish between being *feminine in gender* and being *feminine in form*. Words are feminine in form when they have feminine endings, but they are feminine in gender when they are modified by feminine adjectives. Here are some examples. גְּמַלִּים מֵינִיקוֹת means *nursing camels*; גְּמַלִּים (camels) is a feminine noun with a masculine ending. Many feminine nouns, such as שָׁנָה (year), are formed from roots whose final letter is either ה, or else an original י that has changed to ה. The plurals of such words are normally feminine in gender but masculine in their form, as with שָׁנִים אֲחֵרוֹת (other years). Apparently, when the plural שָׁנִים was formed the third letter—whether it was ה or י—had not yet lost its root-like feeling; but by the time adjectives were distinguished from nouns, the final letter of שָׁנָה had already begun to feel more like a feminine ending.

Many feminine nouns end in a תֶ־ instead of a הָ־. This is known as the *segolite* ending. In many cases both forms exist, often bearing greatly different meanings. The following is a list of those feminine forms that may take the segolite ending.

Old form	New form
קָאטְלַת	קוֹטְלֶת
קְטָאלַת	קְטוֹלֶת
קַטְּלַת	קֻטֶּלֶת
קַטָּאלַת	קְטוֹלֶת

Many words that are clearly feminine both in meaning and in gender are masculine in form:

Feminine		Masculine	
אֵם	Mother	אָב	Father
אָתוֹן	She-ass	חֲמוֹר	He-ass
עֵז	Goat	תַּיִשׁ	Billy goat
רָחֵל	Ewe	אַיִל	Ram
לָבִיא	Lioness	אַרְיֵה	Lion

The fact that so many biologically feminine beings do not have feminine endings has led some writers to infer that the distinction between masculine and feminine is not as fundamental grammatically for the Semitic languages as one might have expected. Some words, like כֶּלֶב, are used in the masculine for all dogs, regardless of sex. Bees, on the other hand, are all regarded as feminine. While there are no strict laws, the following kinds of words tend to be feminine in gender: actions and places, such as the words for *land, city,* and *north,* as well as the names of various countries are typically feminine. Things that are small enough to be held in the hand, such as swords and cups, sandals, buckets, and stones are also feminine, as are the paired parts of the body, such as hands, eyes, ears, and knees. The forces of nature, like the sun, the wind, and light, are feminine, as are those things which we tend to call abstract, such as strength, greatness, and uprightness.[1]

---

1. Jouon, Paul P. *A Grammar of Biblical Hebrew.*

8. The Generation of Verbs

It is customary in Hebrew grammar to take the roots פעל and קטל as paradigmatic for all roots. Each of these two paradigms is used in its own way, קטל for specifying the vocalic mode and פעל for designating the individual root letters. For example, the word אָדָם is said to have the form קָטָל, whereas the noun דָּוִד is said to have the form קְטֹל. On the other hand, in the root אדם, the א is said to be the פ *of the root,* ד is called the ע, and ם is called the ל of the root.

The most primitive words had the form קָטָל. Later they were given a variety of meanings and nuances through two distinctive methods, and it is by means of these that the language grew into what we know as Biblical Hebrew. One of these methods, as we have seen, was to vary the vocalic modes. The other was to conjoin the root with the pronouns. This latter method was done in a myriad of ways, each giving its own kind of nuance. Accordingly, having a fundamental grasp of the Hebrew language is almost identical to understanding the various ways in which the pronouns can attach themselves to the roots, while understanding the significance of each way.

The simplest forms of the verb arose out of the two most basic vocalic patterns, קָטַל and קָטֹל. We shall call the form קָטַל the *solid state,* and the form קָטֹל the *hollow state.*

The solid state spoke of solid things, that is, things as they were, or as they had been. People used the hollow state, on the other hand, to speak about things that were less substantial, such as their dreams and their fears, or their hopes and expectations. Roughly speaking, the solid state is equivalent to the perfect tense in English, while the hollow state is the imperfect. When restated in terms of time, the solid state is usually translated by the English past tense, the hollow state by the English future tense.

As discussed in the previous chapter, the basic pattern קָטַל became קָטָל, whose leaning form was קְטַל. A word like כָּתַב could be closely joined to other words by means of the leaning form, כָּתַב. Such conjunction of words became the foundation of the solid state. For example, כָּתַב conjoined with the word דָּוִד forms the sentence כָּתַב דָּוִד, which means *David is a writing one in the solid state*—or, as we would say, *David wrote*. The leaning form was also conjoined to the pronouns to beget what we know as *verbs*, as indicated in the table below.

The reader should take care to notice where the accent mark falls in the table entries. In Hebrew, the accent generally falls on the last syllable, except for those forms which have retained their final vowel. Remember, when applying this rule, that the 3rd person feminine singular was once כָּתְבַת.

Formation of the Solid State Verb[1]

Singular

כָּתַב	←	—	+	כָּתַב	3rd masc.
כָּתְבָה	←	ת	+	כָּתַב	3rd fem.
כָּתַבְתָּ	←	אַתָּה	+	כָּתַב	2nd masc.
כָּתַבְתְּ	←	אַתְּ	+	כָּתַב	2nd fem.
כָּתַבְתִּי	←	אֲנְתִּי	+	כָּתַב	1st c.

Plural

כָּתְבוּ	←	lengthening	+	כָּתַב	3rd c.
כְּתַבְתֶּם	←	אַתֶּם	+	כָּתַב	2nd masc.
כְּתַבְתֶּן	←	אַתֶּן	+	כָּתַב	2nd fem.
כָּתַבְנוּ	←	אָנוּ	+	כָּתַב	1st c.

As you can see, the verb is merely a contraction of the pronoun and the leaning form of the old verb-like noun. If that contraction had not taken place, it is doubtful whether there would have been any reason at all to speak of verbs when discussing Semitic grammar. This doubtfulness increases when we remember that the two roots אנת and הוה, which form the pronouns, both contain nothing but weak letters. Had that not been the case, it is hard to know whether they would ever have joined with nouns to make up what we look upon as a grammatical form. To that

---

1. In this chart, the stressed syllable is underlined.

extent, one might almost regard the coming-to-be of the verb as being accidental. It is also hard to know whether these conjunctions took place through the exercise of skill, or through laziness on the part of the speakers.

In the preceding chart you can observe a peculiarity we mentioned at the conclusion of Chapter 6—that the third person requires no personal endings. Part of the reason for this is that the subject of a sentence clearly plays the role of the pronoun; for example, compare כָּתַב...תִּי with כָּתַב דָּוִד. On the other hand, a word like כָּתַב can sometimes stand alone, as if in expectation of a subject. When it does, it means *he writes-in-the-solid-state*, that is, *he wrote*. The ending of the third-person feminine is clearly nothing more than the normal feminine ending, but the plural third person might present a puzzle. The ו of the 3rd plural, though at first it may appear to be part of the root הוה, is in fact merely the vestige of an old notion of plurality, as we shall see in the next chapter. It is also interesting to note that the first person requires no distinction in gender, since it is known. The lack of gender in the third person plural, however, is of late origin.

Formation of the Hollow State Verb
Singular

יִכְתֹּב	←	כְּתֹב	+	—	3rd masc.
תִּכְתֹּב	←	כְּתֹב	+	—	3rd fem.
תִּכְתֹּב	←	כְּתֹב	+	אַתָּ	2nd masc.
תִּכְתְּבִי	←	כְּתֹב	+	אַתְּ	2nd fem.
אֶכְתֹּב	←	כְּתֹב	+	אֲנִי	1st c.

Plural

יִכְתְּבוּ	←	כְּתֹב	+	—	3rd masc.
תִּכְתֹּבְנָה	←	כְּתֹב	+	—	3rd fem.
תִּכְתְּבוּ	←	כְּתֹב	+	אַתֶּם	2nd masc.
תִּכְתֹּבְנָה	←	כְּתֹב	+	אַתֶּן	2nd fem.
נִכְתֹּב	←	כְּתֹב	+	אֲנוּ	1st c.

In the case of the hollow state, the pronoun was placed at the beginning and the process of contraction was not quite so straightforward. In the second-person singular, contraction effaced the distinction between feminine and masculine. Thus it was necessary to append the old second-person feminine ending.

Although the י of the third person looks as though it might come from the root הוא, it probably does not. To understand it, we must look more carefully at the contractions involved in the other persons, in order to see where the hireq came from. When אַתָּ and כְּתֹב were contracted, only the תּ remained, leaving a form תְּכְתֹּב. The first syllable, תְּכָ (if one may even call it a syllable) is composed of a resting shewa and a moving shewa. As we have seen in such cases, the first shewa then regularly becomes a hireq. The י in the third-person masculine, then, probably arose as a means of giving substance to the hireq. The final י's and ן's are merely plural forms, as we shall see in the next chapter. The use of the תּ in the third-person plural feminine is of some interest and may be a further indication of an attraction between the feminine and the combined first and second persons, as they are contained in the root אנת.

I noted previously that the Hebrew solid state is often rendered in English as the past tense, and the hollow state as the English future tense. But such translations are only approximate and will not do in all cases. Before considering the matter more deeply, we must first reconsider the English tense system.

As children, we all learned that English has three simple tenses: a past, a present and a future. The past and present tenses seem fairly clear, but the future tense is somewhat hazy. The verb *run* has a perfectly good past tense, *ran*. The past tense in English is formed either by an inner vocalic change or by the addition of the suffix *ed*. But we have no similarly independent future form; instead we use the phrase *he will run*. This way of speaking seems to have arisen in a manner comparable to the expression *he has run*. We all understand that *he has run* is a kind of present tense. That is to say, it speaks about a past experience which the subject presently holds as a past experience. *I did my homework last night* speaks about the way in which I spent those hours. *I have done my homework* implies that I presently possess a certain experience of the past, and am now prepared for class. Odysseus is more than a man who *once saw* "many ways and many lands." He presently is a man who *has seen* "many ways and many lands." This form speaks of the present condition as the result of the past.

In the same manner, *I will go* seems to be a shortened form of the phrase *I will to go*. Originally, it was not an attempt to predict the future, but rather to speak of present animate desires and inanimate tendencies. Perhaps it is partly because the future form has lost its original force that we so often tend to avoid the use of the future altogether. In common speech, we prefer to stick with the present tense by using such forms as *I am going on Wednesday* or *he leaves on Thursday*. Here we have returned to the original sense of the future by speaking about present intention.

Having completed this excursion, which was intended to loosen the tight notion of time that is characteristic of English, let us again turn to the solid and hollow forms as they appear in Hebrew.

The solid state is normally used to speak of things which are complete and over with: "God took him" (Genesis 5:2a). The solid state is sometimes used as we would use the past perfect: to indicate that the over-and-done-with quality of the act had already appeared at some prior time. For example, "Now Samuel was dead, and all Israel mourned him" (I Samuel 28:3). When God asks Cain, "Where is Abel?" Cain answers in the solid state, "I do not know" (Genesis 4:9). In the context, one has no choice but to use the present tense in the English translation; however, Cain's use of the solid state implies that he has never considered his brother to be any of his concern. Similarly, when Isaac speaks of the food "such as I love" (Genesis 27:4) in the solid state, he is speaking of a quality which existed in the past and continues into the present. When Moses says to Pharaoh, "How long wilt thou refuse to humble thyself?" (Exodus 10:3), he too uses the solid state, as if to say, "How long until your refusing is an over-and-done-with thing?" When Gehazi decides to run after the prophet, the English translation rightly reads, "I will run after him" (II Kings 5:20). But Gehazi was so determined to get the money that he spoke in the solid state, as if he had already left; and when David says to Jonathan, "Whatever your heart desires, I will do it" (I Samuel 20:4), he puts the words *I will do it* in the solid state, as though to say, "It is already as good as done." Such constructions as *begone with thee* or *have done with it* were similar modes of speech in Elizabethan times. The prophets, too, often speak of the future as if it were an accomplished fact. Long before its time, Isaiah says, "Therefore my people are gone into captivity."

The hollow state, which grammarians usually call the imperfect, is normally translated as a simple future. Moses said to

God, "they will not believe me" (Exodus 4:1). But the hollow state
may also be used in words of encouragement or indirect
command: "Let the dry land appear" (Genesis 1:9), "Let us turn
into this city and spend the night there" (Judges 19:11). When
used in conjunction with the negative, it is the normal form for
commands, as in "Thou shalt not steal" (Exodus 20:15). The
hollow state, like the English future, is sometimes used in such a
manner as to leave no doubt of its present intention: "I will not
bear your iniquity" (Isaiah 1:13). Questions are often put in the
hollow state to reflect the unfinished character of the unknown:
"What are you looking for?" (Genesis 37:15). Sometimes the
hollow state reflects a spatial rather than a temporal continuum:
"And a river went out of Eden to water the garden; and from
thence it will part and branch into streams" (Genesis 2:10).

The hollow state also came to be used for statements which are
"open" in the sense that they are intended to state something that
is true forever: "A wise son makes a glad father" (Proverbs 15:20).
Consequently, customs are usually expressed in the hollow state:
"And it was a custom in Israel, that the daughters of Israel went
yearly to lament the daughters of Jephtha" (Judges 11:40). When
the angel asks Jacob, "Why ask you my name?" in the hollow state,
one sees immediately that despite the *questioning* being over and
done with, the *question* is not over and done with but will
reverberate through all of time.

In the phrase, "There came a swarm of gnats … and the land
was devastated" (Exodus 8:20), the final verb (to be devastated)
occurs in the hollow state, even though the act is over and done
with from the viewpoint of the book. The effect of this is to allow
the reader to feel the present threat of the gnats.

The hollow state is often used to speak about recurrent
actions, as in Job 1:5: כָּכָה יַעֲשֶׂה אִיּוֹב כָּל־הַיָּמִים, "Thus did Job all
[his] days." Presumably the hollow state is used because of a
certain presupposition that habitual things are not accidental but
presuppose some kind of intention in a larger sense of the word.
The same thought may be contained in the etymological
relationship between the verb *to will* and the English phrase "as
he was wont to do." The Book of Exodus also uses the hollow state
in the phrase "Moses would speak and God would answer him by
voice" (Exodus 19:19). Again, one should note the relation
between the words *would* and *will* as expressing intention, on the
one hand, and desire, on the other.

Hebrew also distinguishes between two groups of verbs in a way that is vaguely related to the difference between transitive and intransitive verbs in English. In Hebrew, קָטַל verbs imply actions and are called *active* verbs; an example is נָתַן, *to give*. The קָטֵל verbs, on the other hand, imply states rather than actions, and they are often referred to as *stative* verbs. As we know from the beginning of Chapter 5, the old *I*-mode vocalics shifted to the *E*-mode; thus the form קָטִל became קָטֵל. Some examples are כָּבֵד, *to be heavy*; טָהֵר, *to be pure*; and חָפֵץ, *to desire*. These verbs sometimes have a form קָטֻל, which becomes קָטֹל; an example is קָטֹן, *to be small*. Some authors say that the קָטֹל verbs tend to reflect more permanent qualities. In any case, the distinction between active and stative verbs exists only in the ground form.

9. The Origins of Number

The formation of the plural in Hebrew is both simple and complicated. The masculine plural ending is ־ִים , while the feminine ending is וֹת. All that remains is to account for them. Unfortunately the history of the masculine plural ending is as complicated as the feminine ending is simple. We must again remind the reader that the use of the words *masculine* and *feminine* applied to a suffix does not necessarily indicate the gender of the word itself.

Akkadian had three cases: nominative, genitive, and accusative. The complete paradigm is as follows:

Declension of the Akkadian Noun

CASE	SINGULAR	PLURAL
	Masculine	
Nom.	טָאבֶּ (ם)	טָאבּוּ
Gen.	טָאבִּ (ם)	טָאבִּי
Acc.	טָאבַּ (ם)	טָאבִּי
	Feminine	
Nom.	טָאבָּתֶ (ם)	טָאבָּתֶוּ (ם)
Gen.	טָאבָּתִ (ם)	טָאבָּתִי (ם)
Acc.	טָאבָּתַ (ם)	טָאבָּתִי (ם)

The ם in parentheses is found only in the earliest stages of the language. It is interesting to note that the letter was primarily used for the singular, though it did appear in the feminine plural. If we neglect the letter ם for now, the Akkadian plural formation becomes quite simple. Each of the three cases ends in a different vowel, and the plurals were formed by transforming that vowel into a consonantal vowel. This is a case of particular interest. It means that some human or half-human in the far distant past had to have been the first to stretch out that final sound in something like hope or expectation that someone else would catch on to the fact the there wasn't just one, but many. We can also notice that in the plural, the genitive ' had already replaced accusative אַ.

In Ugaritic the situation was slightly different. The paradigm looks like this:

Declension of the Ugaritic Noun

CASE	SINGULAR	PLURAL
	Masculine	
Nom.	טָאבֶ	טָאבוֹם
Gen.	טָאבִ	טָאבִים
Acc.	טָאבַ	טָאבִים
	Feminine	
Nom.	טָאבַּתֻ	טָאבָאתֻ
Gen.	טָאבָּתִ	טָאבָאתִ
Acc.	טָאבָּתַ	טָאבָּאתַ

Note that ם has here become a sign of the masculine plural, but the vowel system has remained intact. Again the notion of plurality is being conveyed by lengthening the final vowel— making it "bigger," so to speak. This same device can easily be recognized in the formation of the Hebrew feminine plural, ות. One need only remember that the feminine word, such as אֲדָמָה was once אֲדָמַת; our general rule would lead to a plural אֲדָמָאת which then shifts, as we know from Chapter 4, to אֲדָמוֹת.

In many of the Semitic languages one finds ן forming the plural, rather than ם. The two letters vie with each other throughout the history of the development of the Semitic languages and, as we have already seen, the ן also appears in the feminine plural of the pronoun.

The masculine plural, ים, is more complicated. But if we divide the ending into the two distinct elements ' and ם, we can see in the ' a simple continuation of the process that had already

begun to take place in Akkadian, where the *I*-type consonantal
vowel of the genitive plural (יֵ) had already begun to take over by
devouring the accusative *A*. Accounting for the ם, however, is a
completely separate affair. In our discussion of the concept of
roots in Chapter 5, we saw that roots sometimes tended to come
in clusters. One such cluster may be formed by the letters מ and נ,
appearing in that order. Consider the following roots:

To count, reckon, or number	מָנָה
A part or portion	מָנָה
To give a gift or make an offering	מנח
To withhold or hold back	מנע
From	מִן
What	מָן
Who	מִי [1]
Kind or class	מִין
To refuse or reject	מאן
A special occasion or appointed time	זמן
To hide	טמן
Right	ימן
Fat	שמן
To offer or to shield	מגן

To begin, let us look at מנה, מנח, and מנע. They all have in
common the notion of dividing off one part from another. מנה
simply divides into individuals and therefore allows for *counting*.
מנח, having the softer sounding letter ח, *portions out*; while מנע
with its harsher letter ע closes a part off or *withholds*. From these
words comes the word מִין, a *kind* or a *class*—that is to say, a group
of beings divided off from all other beings. Likewise there arose
the preposition מִן, which means *of* or *from*. From the notion of
dividing comes the word מנה, *manah*, one's daily portion. A *what*,
מן (which will at a later stage transform to מה), or a *who*, מי, is a
thing held up and held apart.

---

1. Although מִי stands out from the other words in this list by not
possessing a נ, its relation to them is revealed in that the word corresponding to it in most other Semitic languages is מָן.

As other letters enter the roots, one finds meanings further removed from the central meaning, but it is still possible to see their connection. An *appointed time* or *occasion* is a time, זמן, that is separated from daily experience. The root מאן, meaning to *refuse*, or *reject*, is not so distant from the root מנע, to *withhold*; nor is the notion of *offering, shielding*, or *protecting* that is found in the word מגן very far from the notion of division. We protect by building walls; we therefore *hide*, טמן, what we divide off and protect.

We can now begin to see in the notion of division the genesis of plurality, and we can also begin to understand the ambiguity which had already begun to appear, and which in a way continues even into Classical Arabic, as to whether the מ\נ belongs more properly to the singular or to the plural. Division can be understood as either making many parts or as singling out one specific part. It is this ambiguity that allows the מ\נ sometimes to signify the singular and sometimes the plural. It is not possible, however, to have a complete picture of the notion of plurality as it expresses itself within the Semitic languages without some understanding of what plurality means for them in its relation to number. A fuller discussion of the problem will be found in the notes to I Samuel 20:5 (Chapter 14 below). Nevertheless, certain general problems can be seen even at this point.

In most cases, the plural is used in Hebrew in exactly the same way as it is in English. That is not true, however, of objects which are counted often and presumably had been counted for many centuries, such as *men, souls, days, years* and *tribes*, and sometimes also for *months, cubits, shekels*, and *cities*. In Hebrew, we say *one window, two windows, nine windows, many windows, or ten windows*; but in those few cases singled out above, we say *one man, two men, nine men, many men*, but *ten man, eleven man*, etc. For these things, anything above ten returns to the singular, and there is every reason to believe that at an earlier stage all plurals worked in this manner. The specific choice of ten is surely related to our fingers and toes, but that does not answer the question why, when numbers are involved, plurality should be limited to small numbers.

Small numbers differ greatly from big numbers. To know that there are a hundred people, I must count each person and arrive at the fact that there are a hundred of them, and that each one of them is a person. But no one ever actually counts three men. One just looks at them and sees that they are three or four or perhaps five. We conclude, therefore, that there are two Semitic notions of plurality. One has its roots in a swarm of manyness and muchness; that side of the matter can be seen in such expressions as *many men*. The other, and perhaps even older, sense of plurality lies in a clear division which allows for the simultaneous recognition of the whole and the multitude of its parts. In this sense, plurality is best captured by seeing an instance of four things as *a single quartet*. This supposition seems not only to account for the strange usage of numbers and for the cluster of roots containing the letters מ and נ, but it also sharpens our understanding of the ambiguous character of נ\מ as pointing sometimes to the singular, as in Akkadian, and sometimes to the plural.

Perhaps even before they learned to group things into definite groups of a definite number of things, when there was only *one* or *many*, people noticed that there were things that were neither one nor many—things like eyes, hands, and lips, a period of two days, and conceivably even a double-wall, although all this probably took place well before there were such things as walls. It wasn't yet numbering, nor even yet counting, but the *pair* was seen as neither one nor many. Below are listed a few Biblical examples, although which ones antedate the numbering system is surely a matter of guesswork. The disposition to see things in pairs has evidently lasted long beyond the coming-to-be of number.

	Singular	*Dual*	*Plural*
Hand	יָד	יָדַיִם	ידות
Foot	רֶגֶל	רַגְלַיִם	רְגָלִים
Ear	אֹזֶן	אָזְנַיִם	
Eye	עַיִן	עֵינַיִם	
Door	דֶּלֶת	דְּלָתַיִם (double doors)	דְּלָתוֹת
Bronze	נְחֹשֶׁת	נְחֻשְׁתַּיִם (fetters)	
Noon		צָהֳרַיִם	

The word for "noon" may have arisen from the root צהר, meaning to *appear* or *mount*. Why is it in the dual form? Perhaps because noon divides daylight into two equal periods. A fuller account of the numbering system and its rise will be given in Chapter 14.

10. I Samuel 20:1

The remainder of this book will be devoted to a close reading of Chapter 20 of The First Book of Samuel. I have chosen it for several reasons. First, the vocabulary is generally rather simple and quite repetitive. Second, it consists of an extended dialogue between David and Jonathan; this choice seemed wise because without dialogue there is neither first nor second person, and since what we know as the third person is virtually taken for granted as the unspoken subject in the Semitic languages, without a living speaker there is hardly any sense of person and precious little grammar.

Before turning to our task, however, we must take an overall look at some of the difficulties we are bound to meet up with. By ill chance, the first verse of the passage we have chosen contains a number of these difficulties, and the author fears that without ample warning the reader may be apt to give up in total despair.

Since Hebrew is much closer to its own origins than are any of the modern Indo-European languages, there are practically no irregular verbs of the sort we are familiar with—verbs such as *am, is, are, be,* etc., which seem to be totally unrelated etymologically even though they are part of the same paradigm. Although this kind of irregularity rarely occurs in Hebrew, there does exist irregularity of another kind.

Irregularities arise when one or more of the three root letters cannot, for euphonic reasons, support the normal vocalic pattern. When one of the root letters is a guttural the difficulties are numerous, and they do not always work according to strict laws. There are, however, essentially three cases of this problem.

1. Gutturals tend to reject the shewa state and replace it with one of the ḥatuphim: not יְעֲשֶׂה but יַעֲשֶׂה (see Chapter 5).

2. Gutturals tend to attract the *A* mode: פַּעַם, where one might have expected פֶּעַם.

3. They reject the dagesh: הָאָזֵל, not הַאָזֵל.

Some of the guttural letters exhibit greater attraction for the *A* mode than do others. The order of preference is: ע > ח > ה > א;

however, one cannot speak of laws here, but only of general tendencies.

Although neither the gutturals nor the letter ר can accept a dagesh, they sometimes act as they if they had accepted the dagesh. Compare the word יְדַבֵּר with the word יְבַעֵר. The two words have the same form, except that while the בּ in יְדַבֵּר has accepted the dagesh which is proper to the form, the ע has rejected it. The דַ in the word יְדַבֵּר is pronounced in the short mode because the syllable has been closed by the dagesh in the בּ. However, the בַ in the word יְבַעֵר is also pronounced in the short mode, even though the ע has rejected the dagesh. One might say that the ע has accepted a *virtual* dagesh. Again, one may only speak of a letter's general tendency to accept a virtual dagesh. The order of this tendency is: ר > א > ע > ח > ה.

The next problem is that the letters א, ו, and י, even when they are part of a root, tend to degenerate into consonantal vowels; and that when נ appears in the resting shewa mode it is devoured by the letter that follows it. Thus יְמוּת, from the root מות, becomes יָמֻת; and יִנְשָׁק becomes יִשַּׁק, where the dagesh in the שּׁ is the ghost of the devoured נ.

For most gutturals these difficulties arise in any of the three root positions, though there are exceptions. In the following chart a mark (×) indicates where a difficulty has to be resolved:

	ל	ע	פ
Gutturals	×	×	×
א	×		×
ו	×	×	×
י	×	×	×
נ	×		

The only additional difficulty is that in some roots the second and third letters are identical, as in סבב. These cases too we must learn to handle with special care. This brief discussion was only intended to give the reader an overall view of the situation, and we will develop each particular case as it arises in our reading.

Now on to the task. Since there is still much grammar to be learned, the notes will tend to be rather long at first. They will, however, dwindle in scope and number as the reader begins to take over.

Although the notes do not presuppose that the reader has acquired a Biblical Hebrew dictionary or lexicon, it will be very useful to have one at hand.

I Samuel 20:1

1 וַיִּבְרַח דָּוִד מִנָּוֹת [מִנָּיוֹת] בָּרָמָה וַיָּבֹא וַיֹּאמֶר | לִפְנֵי יְהוֹנָתָן מֶה עָשִׂיתִי מֶה־עֲוֹנִי וּמֶה־חַטָּאתִי לִפְנֵי אָבִיךָ כִּי מְבַקֵּשׁ אֶת־נַפְשִׁי׃

Notes to the reading:

וַיִּבְרַח דָּוִד

Except for the ו in וַיִּבְרַח, the reader should recognize the form. Note also that the vocalic mode of the ר has switched to the *A* mode under the influence of the guttural ח. The main transformation is: יִבְרַח ← יִבְרֹח

The root ברח means *to flee*. The meaning of דָּוִד we leave to the reader's ingenuity

The ו attached to the word וַיִּבְרַח is a general connective, roughly meaning *and*; but its effect is rather complicated. I believe, however, that understanding that complication may be key to understanding the distinction between the hollow form and the solid form. The present account is based on the insight of P. Paul Jouon as found in his *Grammaire de l'Hebreu Biblique*.

Jeremiah 20:13 states אָכַל וְשָׁתָה, which means *he ate and he drank*. Had the text read יֹּאכַל וַיִּשְׁתֶּה, it would have meant *he will eat and he will drink*. Thus far things are much as one might have expected, though one should note here and try to understand the vocalic effect of the א.

But now consider the sentence אָכַל וַיִּשְׁכַּב, where the root שכב means *to lie down*. Here the author has conjoined two verbs which differ in modality. The sentence as a whole, however does not mean *He ate and he will lie down*, but rather *He ate and then he lay down*. In this case one can see that the lying down came immediately after, and perhaps as a consequence of, the eating. In other words, the lying down is imperfect, or *hollow*, in the sense of being an expectation or an as yet unfulfilled goal—not from the point of view of the speaker, but rather from the point of view of the eating. In the same way, יֹאכַל וּשָׁכַב came to mean *He will eat and go right to sleep.*

At times the force of the ו can be even stronger, as in the sentence אָכַל וַיְחִי, *He ate in order that he might live.* In most cases, however, the ו has very little effect, and the phrase אָכַל וַיִּשְׁתֶּה simply translates as *he ate and drank.* This mode of expression became so common that eventually the word וַיִּשְׁתֶּה standing by itself, even with no other verb to precede, was still taken to mean *And he drank* and not *And he will drink.* However, one wonders whether somewhere behind this way of speaking there might not lie the vague notion that things mostly occur within a context, either articulated or left unarticulated. The waw in our word וַיִּבְרַח functions in this way, to yield "And David fled...." Some grammarians call it *waw consecutive*, although it rarely *follows* anything.

מִנָּווֹת [מִנָּיוֹת]

Although the received Hebrew text has מִנָּווֹת, it is traditional to read מִנָּיוֹת instead. In this and similar cases, the text as received is called כתיב (Aramaic: *written*); the traditional reading, here enclosed in square brackets, is called קרי (Aramaic: *read*).

נָיוֹת (Naioth) is the name of a city. Its exact location is not certain. The dagesh in the נ of מִנָּיוֹת represents a dropped letter; fully expressed, the text would have read מִן נָיוֹת. As we have seen, מִן is a preposition meaning *from*, and probably coming from the root מנה, *to divide.* This might suggest that in very ancient times, one would have said: בָּרַח דָּוִד מָנָה נָיוֹת, a rough translation of which might read: *David fled, departing Naioth.*

Prepositions, even though they were handed to us when we were children, are very sophisticated beings. *Of* is not a phenomenon or an object like a table, or even like the act of singing. It was not just there, but had to be arrived at by human thought. That means that an act of human thought lies within our own daily speech and modes of thinking which we ourselves have never thought. To that extent we lack self-understanding. It is this situation that makes it necessary for us to go back with such care in order to get a clearer glimpse of ourselves, and of the things we thoughtlessly take for granted.

בָּרָמָה

To make this word intelligible, we shall have to break it up in a rather strange way: בָּ-רָמָה. The word is a crasis for בְּהָרָמָה. The word רָמָה is a feminine noun, the masculine of which would be רָם. A bit of scurrying about the dictionary would reveal a root רום, meaning *high* or *exalted.* This exercise gives us our first taste of how one deals with an irregular root. The word רָוָם becomes רָם. The feminine, רָמָה, means *height* or *heights*—in the sense of a hill, or an elevated or hilly region.

The בּ is a proclitic equivalent to our preposition *in.* Its origins are unclear, but a fuller account will be given in Chapter 19, below.

This leaves the question of the implied הָ. It is the definite article *the,* but to understand it we must see it in its more normal environment. The word for *old man* is זָקֵן. *The old man* would be הַזָּקֵן. Here the dagesh implies an earlier form הַן זָקֵן, or an even older form הַנַּ זָקֵן. In the case of our word, בְּהָרָמָה or בָּרָמָה, all of this is hidden because the ר has rejected the dagesh. Etymologically, the word is related to such words as הֵנָּה which means *here* or *hither* and to הִנֵּה, a word which calls attention to what is present. King James's men often translate it *behold,* but its force is seen more clearly in expressions such as *here am I.* As in the Romance, Germanic, and Greek languages, the definite article seems to be a weakened form of the demonstrative, just as in English, *the* is a weakened form of *this.*

In the word הָרָמָה or *the heights,* the definite article has a particularly interesting force. When people in Los Angeles speak of The Valley, it goes without saying that they mean the San Joaquin Valley. Similarly, הרמה was the name of a specific *Height* in Benjamin, sometimes simply known as רמה.

וַיָּבֹא

The root is בוא, meaning *to come.* As the reader can see, there are two implied difficulties, one because of the וֹ, the other because of the א. However, since there happen to be so many irregular roots in this verse, we shall defer the full discussion to a later occasion. Note again the force of the וֹ, yielding the translation "and he came."

וַיֹּאמֶר

The root אמר has an א in the פ position (grammarians therefore call it a "פ-א" root). The fundamental transformation is:

$$יֹאמֶר \leftarrow יְאֳמֶר .$$

Here one can see that א reveals its vocalic characteristic in the hollow state. Recalling the original form, we can see that it would ordinarily transform to יְאֳמֶר. Under the influence of the א, however, it becomes יַאֳמֶר instead. Then the א is taken as vocalic, and we have יָאמֶר, which, as we know, would normally have led to יֹמַר or יוֹמַר. In this case, though, since the א is one of the root letters it was retained in the written word but has no other significance—hence it has no vocalic mode.

In general, the best way of grasping an irregular form is to articulate what the regular form would have been, and then try to get a feeling for the euphonics involved. This will require experience, since euphony clearly changes from language to language, from age to age, and often from block to block.

The root אמר means *to say (something)*. In other words, like the word *say* (as opposed to the word *to speak*) it demands a direct object. The root may have been derived from a more fundamental meaning, *to be bright* or *to make visible*—or even *be or make prominent*, as if the prime task of speech were to help people make the various facets of the world visible to one another.

לִפְנֵי יְהוֹנָתָן

To be understood, the first word must be broken into two parts: לְ-פְנֵי. The לְ, which is equivalent to the English preposition *to*, is a separable prefix that often appears as the word אֶל (*to*) or עַל (*on*). These both derive from the root עלה, which means *to go up* or *to mount or ascend*.

Let us try to gain some insight into the transition from עלה to עַל. Perhaps someone among the earliest speakers innately felt that the words הוא עלה הר—*he ascends a mountain*—did not quite grasp his thought. He may have shortened it to הוא על הר—*he is on a mountain*—thinking that others might catch on. Of course any such venture must have taken place long before proto-Semitic broke up into its various branches about six thousand years ago. But it may have been some such floundering as this that led to the sophisticated notion of a *preposition*.

When used in the sense of *on* (or the more aggressive sense of *against*), the root עלה tends to retain the harsh-sounding ע to become the *preposition* עַל. When used in the gentler senses of *to* or *towards*, it tends to drop the ע and become simply לְ or אֶל. In actual practice, one can only speak of a general tendency to drop the ע under more gentle circumstances, and no universal law can be given. Some scholars have been led to conclude that the distinction between gentle and harsh is irrelevant, but I find that opinion to be itself too harsh.

The remaining part of the word, פְּנֵי, is a leaning plural of which the absolute form is פָּנִים, and it leans on the word יְהוֹנָתָן. Its root, פנה, may have first meant *to turn away from* or even *to banish,* but it gradually acquired the meaning *to send towards* or *to turn in a given direction.*

The word פָּנִים means *face.* It always occurs in the plural, perhaps because of symmetry of the face, perhaps because of the manifold of characteristics that it can show at different times. A difficulty yet remains in that one may speak of *the face of a building,* but it is not clear whether we intend that part of the building that we look at, or the part that looks at us.

Although לִפְנֵי is crasis of אֶל פְּנֵי, in this particular case some distinction must be made. אֶל פְּנֵי retains its literal meaning, *to* or *in* the face of, whereas לִפְנֵי has the more detached meaning of *before,* either in a spatial or a temporal sense.

At this point the reader should be able to account for the missing kamaṣ (ָ) under the פ, and for the ḥireq (ִ) under the ל.

מֶה

The word מֶה was originally מָן, meaning *what;* it belongs to that cluster of roots discussed in the previous chapter. מָן conjoins with other words in very much the same way that the definite article does, except that it retains a greater independence. Thus, the question מָן זֶה becomes מַה־זֶּה. Here the dagesh in the ז is all that remains of the נ. The hyphen-like line, called a *maqqef,* is not always used; and although the ה is always vocalic in this word, one can find מַה as well as מֶה. In our phrase מֶה־עֲוֹנִי, however, the ע has rejected the dagesh; but the מה, instead of becoming the totally independent word מָה, continues to behave as if it were a part of the following syllable, that is, as if the segol (ֶ) were some kind of hatuph.

עָשִׂיתִי

The root עשׂי means *to do* or *to make.* The shifts are

$$עֲשִׂיתִי \leftarrow עָשִׂיתִי$$
$$עֲשִׂי \leftarrow עָשָׂה$$

In the solid mode, as the reader can see, the י tends to assert its vocalic character, affecting the mode of the preceding letter so that we have עָשִׂיתִי where we would have expected עֲשִׂיתִי. If that effect had been consistent, the 3rd masc. sing. would have been עָשִׂי or perhaps עֲשִׂי; but since these forms no longer have the ring of a verb, the patah (ַ) won out over the י and the word became עָשָׂה. For this reason most traditional grammar books call עָשָׂה a ל-ה verb instead of a ל-י verb. Note, by the way, that the ה has lengthened the mode of the שׂ.

מֶה־עֲוֹנִי

Semitic roots give rise to nouns as well as verbs. The root עוה —or more correctly, עוי—means *to be twisted* or *bent,* and hence *to act crookedly* or *perversely.* Nouns were formed from these roots both by tweaking the vocalic pattern and by adding a מ or ת to the beginning or a נ to the end. It is often helpful to compare such nouns with others having the same vocalic pattern.

The vocalic pattern of our word is a transformation of קְטָלָאן; that is, the word would have been עֲוָיָאן, but since the vocalic אָ went to וֹ and the final vowel (ַ)was dropped it became עֲוִיוֹן. Then the law of lightening together with euphonic considerations led to עָוֹן.

The origin of the noun forms is somewhat obscure. However, the fact that the added letters מ, נ, and ת all happen to be letters used in the formation of the pronoun tempts one to look for a fuller account. The vocalic pattern apparently goes back to a similar pattern קָטָלָאַן in Akkadian, where it is normally used as a diminutive. Perhaps it is not too rash to suspect that there might have been a certain connection between the first person and the diminutive, as it reveals itself in such expressions as "my little chickadee"; for in general we tend to use the diminutive for those things for which we feel some close attachment. In Hebrew, however, the form has lost any sense of the diminutive it might once have had.

The word itself means a *perversion* or *transgression.* Other words having the same form are:

Root		Word	
זכר	remember	זִכָּרוֹן	a memory
חזה	see (poetic)	חָזוֹן	a vision
חרה	burn	חָרוֹן	fury
בטח	trust	בִּטָחוֹן	security

The final י in the word עֲוֹנִי is also part of the first-person pronoun, and represents yet another way in which the pronouns attach themselves to roots.

These endings may attach themselves either to nouns in the leaning form or to verbs, though in some cases the verbal endings are not identical to the nominal endings. When added to a verb, they play the role of a direct object; when added to a nouns, they denote possession. If we recall that the distinction between nouns and verbs in the Semitic languages is somewhat superficial, the similarity should not be surprising. In other words, pre-Biblical Hebrew may have felt no need to distinguish between *He is my shepherd,* and *He shepherds me.*

When the word to which the endings are added ends in an open syllable, the endings are as shown in Tables 10.1 and 10.2.

Note that since final ה is generally not pronounced, a dot, called a *mappiq,* is placed in the הָ of the 3rd person feminine to

Objective Endings for Verbs
Possessive Endings for Singular Nouns

Plural			Singular			
Verbs	Common	Nouns	Verbs	Common	Nouns	
ם		הֶם\מוֹ		הוּ		3rd masc.
ן		הֶן		הָ\־ָה		3rd fem.
	כֶם			ךָ		2nd masc.
	כֶן			ךְ		2nd fem.
	נוּ		נִי		־ִי	1st c.

Table 10.1

Possessive Endings for Plural Nouns

Plural	Singular	
‎ֶ־יהֶם	‎ְ־יו	3rd masc.
‎ֶ־יהֶן	‎ֶ־יהָ	3rd fem.
‎ֶ־יכֶם	‎ֶ־יךָ	2nd masc.
‎ַ־יכֶן	‎ַ־יִךְ	2nd fem.
‎ֵ־ינוּ	‎ַ־י	1st c.

Table 10.2

indicate that it is to be pronounced. The mappiq distinguishes in sound between סוּסָה, *a mare*, and סוּסָהּ, *her stallion*.

The origins of the forms listed in the tables should be fairly clear to the reader, but perhaps it should be noted that when the first and second persons were originally differentiated from each other, the כ of the alternative form אנך became the foundation for the second person. It should also be noted that for singular nouns and verbs that end in a closed syllable, a connective vocalic sound was often felt to be necessary. Its use seems never to have become fixed, but shows a great deal of variation within the Biblical text.

Thus, returning to our text, the word עֲוֹנִי means *my perversion*.

וּמֵה־חַטָּאתִי

The root חטא means *to miss* a way or a goal; and hence *to transgress*. חַטָּאת is feminine, and of the form קַטֶלֶת. When the final vocalic sound was dropped the general case became קַטֶלְת, as one might have expected. As we have seen before in the masculine, the patah (ַ)was split up into two segols, (ֶ ֶ). Note also that segol lacks the force that would allow the ת to become a ה. In our case, however, the א became vocalic, and חַטָּאֶת became חַטָּאת. The masculine form would have been קַטָּל.

This form reveals yet another way in which the basic form קטל was modified to capture more accurately the intended meaning. Here the critical change is the doubling of the middle root letter, and its force is to strengthen the meaning of the root notion. Sometimes the change is slight; sometimes it is profound.

Like קַטֵל, the form קַטָּל will serve as the basis of yet another complete form of the verb, including both a solid and a hollow

state, We shall call it the *forceful level*. For instance, the root שָׁבַר
means *he broke*. The forceful level would have been שָׁבַּר. However,
the law of lightening sends it to שָׁבַּר and hence to שָׁבֵּר, which
means *he smashed*.

Even in Biblical times these forms had already become rigid
and could not be made up on the spot with any expectation of
being understood. Although flexibility and inventiveness must
have marked the language at one stage, meanings gradually
became fixed and hardened, often in quite specific directions.
For example, לָמַד means *to learn*, but לִמֵּד means *to teach*. While
one can usually follow the insight that led to each particular
formation, they cannot in general be guessed in advance. In our
case, the simple form חטא itself has developed the stronger sense
of *sin* or *transgression* and thus does not differ greatly from the
forceful level.

חַטָּאת is a noun. When we come to the verbal form, we will
play closer attention to the vocalic changes involved.

לִפְנֵי אָבִיךָ

The word אָב means *father*, but it seems to have a somewhat
wider scope. The phrase, *father of those that handle the harp*,
probably did not sound quite as metaphorical in Hebrew as it
does in English. The root was probably אבי and first meant *he who
decides*, but there is also a second root in Hebrew אבה which
means *to be willing* or *to desire*. The leaning form is usually אַב but
אֲבִי does occur. At any rate, as we have seen in the case of עשי,
the word was later felt to have once been אָבָה. As so often
happens in the case of masculine words that end in ֶה, that
ending was dropped in the singular; but because of the original
form, the plural became אָבוֹת—as if the old ֶה ending had been
a feminine ending.

כִּי

כִּי appears to be a member of the root cluster, mentioned in
Chapter 5, that centers around the root כון, *to be firm and upright*,
and hence simply *to exist*. From there, the word כִּי seems to have
diverged off in the direction of being a demonstrative. One can
still see that in verses like:

> And Judah said unto his brethren, "What profit [is it] *that* we
> slay our brother, and conceal his blood?" (Genesis 37:26)

Here one sees the trace of an older time when one would have said: "What profit is *this*: we slay our brother, and conceal his blood?" In fact our own word *that* underwent the very same transformation.

Like other words in the cluster, כִּי begins by meaning something like *thus*, but shades off into the somewhat stronger meaning *surely*, as in the verse

> And Joab said, As God lives, unless you had spoken, *surely then* in the morning the people would have gone up everyone from following his brother. (II Samuel 2:27)

In its most advanced stages, כִּי almost comes to mean *because*:

> And the Lord God said to the serpent, Because you have done this, you are cursed above all cattle, and above every beast of the field. (Genesis 3:14)

The introductory nature of this book will not allow for a fuller inquiry into the word כִּי, but since the notion of cause and effect is taken so much for granted in the world, such a serious inquiry should be undertaken by each of us. In that way we may hope to see the modes of thought that we received unthinkingly as having arisen out of unreflective, yet nonetheless human, thought in the face of the things that are at hand. Only then can we call such modes of thought truly our own.

מְבַקֵּשׁ

If we divide the word up into its parts מְ and בַקֵּשׁ, we can see that it is related to the forceful level. In fact, the root בקשׁ exists only in the forceful level.

The original form of the forceful level was probably just קַטַל. If we spell that out as קַטַטַל, we can see that the law of lightening would have led to קַטַּל and hence to קַטֵּל or קִטֵּל. As we have seen, the *A* vocalic mode is the most fundamental. It is, therefore, the least specific in meaning, and hence the most open to euphonic change. Thus under the influence of the ֵ , the ַ went to ִ . The paradigms are shown in Table 10.3.

The מ in מְבַקֵּשׁ is a shred of the word מִי, the interrogative pronoun *who*, mentioned in Chapter 9. Unlike the English word *who*, מִי never fully became a relative pronoun in Biblical Hebrew; but one can see how close it had come to doing so in the verse מִי־הָאִישׁ אֲשֶׁר בָּנָה בַיִת־חָדָשׁ וְלֹא חֲנָכוֹ יֵלֵךְ וְיָשֹׁב לְבֵיתוֹ (Deuteronomy 20:5). Here one might attempt to render מִי as a

Forceful Level of the Simple Form

Hollow		Solid		
Plural	Singular	Plural	Singular	
יַקְטְלוּ	יַקְטֵל	קִטְלוּ	קָטַל	3rd masc.
תְּקַטֵּלְנָה	תְּקַטֵּל	קִטְלוּ	קָטְלָה	3rd fem.
תְּקַטְּלוּ	תְּקַטֵּל	קְטַלְתֶּם	קָטַלְתָּ	2nd masc.
תְּקַטֵּלְנָה	תְּקַטְּלִי	קְטַלְתֶּן	קָטַלְתְּ	2nd fem.
נְקַטֵּל	אֲקַטֵּל	קָטַלְנוּ	קָטַלְתִּי	1st c.

Table 10.3

relative pronoun by translating: *Whoever the man is who has built a new house and has not dedicated it, let him go and return to his house.* Nevertheless the verse does not completely escape a sense of *finding*, and hence of *looking for* such a man; and in fact some translators render the מִי interrogatively, as: "*What man is there who has built a new house, and has not dedicated it? Let him go...*" I suggest that in this example מִי lies somewhere between an interrogative and a relative, and that such verses help us grasp how transitions occur in language. In Post-Biblical Hebrew מִי, like the English *who*, is both an interrogative and a relative pronoun.

The root בקשׁ means *to seek out*. The whole word thus means *he who seeks*, and it serves as the Hebrew equivalent of the participle in the forceful level (Table 10.4).

Fundamentally, participles are nouns and might rather be called *actor nouns*. They have noun-like endings rather than the verb-like personal endings and they can take a definite article; for example, הַמְּבַקֵּשׁ means *the one who is seeking*. But participles also have a verbal character. They can take an object, or at least they can seem to do so. The sentence הוּא מְבַקֵּשׁ אֱמֶת can mean either *He is seeking truth* or *He is a seeker of truth*; in

Participle of the Forceful Level

Plural		Singular		
Leaning	Simple	Leaning	Simple	
מְקַטְּלֵי	מְקַטְּלִים	מְקַטֵּל	מְקַטֵּל	Masc.
מְקַטְּלוֹת	מְקַטְּלוֹת	מְקַטֶּלֶת	מְקַטֶּלֶת	Fem.

Table 10.4

other words, מְבַקֵּשׁ can either be the simple form with אֱמֶת as
the direct object, or it can be the leaning form, leaning on the
word אֱמֶת.

The participle or actor noun of the ground form is a simple
noun having the form קָאטֵל. Under the general laws of vocalic
shift, the form became קוֹטֵל. The full paradigm is:

Declension of the Active Participle

	Singular	*Plural*
masc.	קוֹטֵל	קוֹטְלִים
fem.	קוֹטֶלֶת	קוֹטְלוֹת

A participle's meaning is strictly tied to the verbal meaning
of its root. Other nouns, by contrast, often take on highly
specific meanings that stray far from the root meanings. For
this reason the dictionary definition of each noun must be
looked up separately. Nouns are listed in the dictionary or
lexicon under their roots. To help identify the root, recall what
I mentioned earlier: that nouns were formed partly by variation
in the vocalic pattern of the root, and partly by addition of a נ
or ת or מ.

You can see how the participle may function similarly to our
present tense. Consider the phrase *He is seeking*. We often brush
it aside by calling it the progressive tense of the verb, but perhaps
it would be better to consider the word *seeking* in that phrase as
something more nounlike: *He is a seeking-one*, that is, *he seeks*.
Although English would still distinguish between these two
constructions, Hebrew does not. In English we would distinguish
between *He lives at 880 Peerless Avenue* and *He is living at 880
Peerless Avenue*. The latter has a more temporary feel to it. That
temporary quality is what gives the participle its present-
tense-like flavor.

אֶת

There is no English equivalent to the word אֶת. While its usage
is simple and quite straightforward, an adequate understanding of
the word will require a somewhat arduous and detailed account.
Like English, Hebrew dropped the notion of case for the noun
but retained it in the pronoun. We have already learned the
nominative forms of the pronoun; the forms for the direct object
are listed in Table 10.5.

Objective Pronouns

Plural	Singular	
אֶתְהֶם \ אֹתָם	אֹתוֹ	3rd masc.
אֶתְהֶן \ אֹתָן	אֹתָהּ	3rd fem.
אֶתְכֶם	אֹתְךָ	2nd masc.
*	אֹתָךְ	2nd fem.
אֹתָנוּ	אֹתִי	1st c.

* No 2nd fem. plural objective pronoun appears in the Biblical text.

Table 10.5

As we can see, these forms are nothing more than the personal endings attaching themselves to the word אֵת. But to understand the word אֵת itself, it will help to look at the situation as it appears in Akkadian. The curiosity that sends us off in this direction is that אֵת looks too close to the second person to be accidental, and yet on the surface there seems to be no special relationship between the direct object and the second person. This is the oddity that sends us scrambling.

Akkadian, unlike Hebrew, has not one but two sets of objective pronouns. One set is used for the direct object; the other is used for the indirect object. The paradigms are given in Table 10.6.

If we confine our attention to the direct object things start to look somewhat familiar, especially when we remember that while Akkadian shares with Hebrew the root אנת \ אנכ, the third person pronoun in Akkadian is שׁוּא rather than הוּא. Here too we find את plus a form of the pronoun, though the order is reversed. That is to say, in Akkadian the person, שׁ, כ, or נ \ י precedes the ת instead of following it.

Akkadian Objective Pronouns

Indirect		Direct		
Plural	Singular	Plural	Singular	
שָׁנוּשִׁי(ם)	שָׁאֲשִׁי(ם)	שָׁנוּתִי	שָׁאָתִי	3rd masc.
שְׁנָאשִׁי(ם)	שָׁאֲשִׁי(ם)	שְׁנָאתִי	שָׁאָתִי	3rd fem.
כְּנֻשִׁי(ם)	כָּשִׁי(ם)	כְּנֻתִי	כָּתִי	2nd masc.
כְּנָאשִׁי(ם)	כָּשִׁי(ם)	כְּנָאתִי	כָּתִי	2nd fem.
נָאשִׁי(ם)	יְשִׁי(ם)	נָאתִי	יָתִי	1st c.

Table 10.6

The interesting difference is that while the Akkadian direct object continues to show an affinity to the second person, the indirect object, with its use of the suffix שׁ, is related to the third person. In other words, the Akkadian direct object is the object which the actor, or perhaps even the verb itself, faces directly as a "you," while it treats the indirect object indirectly as a third person. One might say that the direct object is a second person, not from the point of view of the speaker, but from the point of view of the actor.

In our verse, the word אֵת has conjoined itself to a noun rather than to a pronoun. The parallel may be closer than at first appears, since the ancients saw no need to put spaces between what we think of as individual words. The word אֵת is used whenever the direct object is a definite object that can be directly faced as a second person. Thus it is used with proper nouns, or with nouns that are qualified either by the definite article or by a possessive ending, for example: *David, the field,* or *my father.* אֵת would appear in the sentence *Therefore you shall deal kindly with your servant,* but not in the sentence *Therefore you shall deal kindly with a servant.*

נַפְשִׁי

In Akkadian the root means *to enlarge,* but even there it was used particularly of the chest; hence it came to mean *to breathe.* According to many scholars, the Hebrew word נֶפֶשׁ often means *throat,* but so far as I have been able to determine, it is never used unambiguously in that mundane sense; no one ever had a bone stuck in his נֶפֶשׁ. A few such appearances of נֶפֶשׁ are:

> Therefore Sheol hath enlarged her נֶפֶשׁ, and opened her mouth without measure (Isaiah 5:14)
>
> All the labor of man is for his mouth, and yet the נֶפֶשׁ is not filled. (Ecclesiastes 6:7)
>
> My נֶפֶשׁ shall be satisfied as with marrow and fatness; and my mouth shall praise you with joyful lips (Psalm 63:6)

Sometimes even an animal's blood is referred to as its נֶפֶשׁ, but only when, and perhaps only insofar as, the blood is looked on as vital to its existence. Even there, it is not clear whether the נֶפֶשׁ is the *blood,* or the *vitality.*

> But flesh with its life (נֶפֶשׁ), which is its blood, you shall not eat. (Genesis 9:4)

I hesitate to offer a definition of the word נֶפֶשׁ, but will instead leave you to the dictionaries, and to your own reflections.

11. I Samuel 20:2

2 וַיֹּאמֶר לוֹ חָלִילָה לֹא תָמוּת הִנֵּה לוֹ [לֹא] ־עֲשֶׂה
[יַעֲשֶׂה] אָבִי דָּבָר גָּדוֹל אוֹ דָּבָר קָטֹן וְלֹא יִגְלֶה אֶת־אָזְנִי
וּמַדּוּעַ יַסְתִּיר אָבִי מִמֶּנִּי אֶת־הַדָּבָר הַזֶּה אֵין זֹאת׃

Notes on the Reading:

וַיֹּאמֶר לוֹ

Note that ל and אֶל, like other prepositions, may also take personal endings. These endings may or may not go back to the time when the prepositions were nouns and verbs. It is hard to tell at this point, but a more complete account will be found in Chapter 20.

חָלִילָה

The noun comes from the root חלל, meaning *to undo a knot*. In Arabic, the word reflects a certain duality; it can mean either *to become free from obligation* or *to desecrate*. In Hebrew it came to mean *to profane*. This particular form, קְטִילַת, has a somewhat abstract, somewhat passive sense.

In the masculine form, one finds words like:

Root		Noun	
שׂכר	to hire	שָׂכִיר	a hired laborer
צער	to be insignificant	צָעִיר	a youth
הלך	to walk	הֲלִיכָה	a march
סלח	to forgive	סְלִיחָה	forgiveness

חָלִילָה is universally used as an expletive meaning something like *Far be it from....* It probably derives from an original notion such as *It would be profane to....*

לֹא

לֹא is a general negative found in most of the Semitic languages and used mainly with verbs, for example:

He did not make   לֹא עָשָׂה

He will not make   לֹא יַעֲשֶׂה

Just as in English, the negation of the imperfect can have the force of a negative command:

You will not make / Do not make!   לֹא תַעֲשֶׂה

The origins of לֹא are unknown. Some writers suppose the א to be part of the old accusative ending. If this is the case (which to me does not seem likely) we have only the ל to work with. Others suppose that לֹא is a metathesis of the word אַל, another negative, used only in negative commands. The patach (ַ) in אַל would seem to suggest that the original came from a root אלל. There does in fact exist a word אֱלִיל, meaning *insufficiency* or *worthlessness*.

It is particularly unfortunate that no one has been able to uncover the roots of this word, since it would be of great importance to our proper task to know whether negation has its deepest origins in an inner feeling of revulsion, or in the perception of a lack or an emptiness in the world about us. Little more can be said until we can contrast it with the other main term for negation, אַיִן, which will appear at the end of the verse.

תָּמוּת

The root is מות, and it is irregular because of the ו. The best way to understand an irregular word is to write out the normal form, then try to figure out and understand what transformations have taken place. The old form of the 2nd masculine singular would have been תַּמְוָאת. This, as we have learned, becomes תַּמְוֹות. The ו then becomes vocalic and we have תָּמוּת.

The root מות means *death*. It may or may not be related to the Latin word *mortus,* and hence to the English word *mortal.* In Greek the word appears as *brotos,* meaning a mortal as opposed to the gods, and also appears in the word am-brosia, the food of the deathless ones. We mortals, because we are mortal, or *brotos,* are dependent on substantial food, mainly on bread, or as it appears in German, *brot,* which also comes from the same Greek root.

הִנֵּה

This word, which King James' men often translate as "behold," is a form of the old demonstrative pronoun and is related to the definite article, the נ of which persists here as the dagesh. It is a near kin to the word הֵנָּה, where the ‑ָה is the old accusative ending mentioned earlier and which means *hither,* or *to this place,* as in

> But in the fourth generation they shall come *here* again; for the iniquity of the Amorites is not yet full. (Genesis 15:16)

Our form, הִנֵּה, strongly points to the here and present. It is typical of the word that, when Pharaoh says to Abram:

> Why did you say, She is my sister? so I might have taken her for my wife; now therefore *here is* your wife, take her, and go your way (Genesis 12:19),

he intends to be forcing Abram to face the situation. The word can also conjoin with the personal pronouns, so that when Abraham uses the word הִנֵּנִי in the verse:

> And it came to pass after these things, that God tested Abraham, and said to him, Abraham; and he said, *Behold, here I am* (Genesis 22:1),

he intends to imply more than his mere physical presence; he is affirming his sense of readiness.

אֲבִי דָּבָר

According to some scholars, the root דבר originally meant *to buzz,* from which comes the word, דְּבוֹרָה *a buzzing one* or *a bee.* In Biblical Hebrew the verbal form means *to speak.* In contrast to the word אמר, which originally meant *to shed light* but which for the most part now means *to say,* דבר does not require a direct object, whereas the word אמר does. As in English, one may *speak,* simply; but one must *say* something.

In the Bible one often finds the phrase וַיְדַבֵּר לֵאמֹר which is traditionally translated *and he spoke, saying.* In this phrase there is still some pale reflection of the original sense of the two words. The phrase reveals the dual character of human speech. Those who first used the word אמר to refer to human speech must have felt that their arbitrary buzzings were in effect shedding light on the things that surround them. One might playfully translate וַיְדַבֵּר לֵאמֹר as: "*And he buzzed, indicating...*"

Other scholars connect the root דבר to the Arabic root which originally meant *to go away,* or *to perish*—whence, they argue, arises the Hebrew דֶּבֶר, meaning *plague.* Later the root acquired the meaning *to lead away.* To me this seems somewhat unlikely, but I can offer no more persuasive alternative.

The word דָּבָר that appears in our text has an intriguing ambiguity. When Moses says "I am not a man of דְּבָרִים" he clearly means "I am not a man of speech." On the other hand, the word can also encompass meanings such as *matter* or even *thing*, as in the following verses:

> When they have a *matter*, they come to me; and I judge between one and another, and I make them know the statutes of God, and his laws. (Exodus 18:16)

and

> Hurry, escape there; for I can not do *any thing* till you come there. (Genesis 19:22)

We also frequently come upon the phrase, "And it came to pass after these דְּבָרִים" (after these things). The Greek word *logos* means both "speech" and "thought"; one might say in a similar spirit that דבר means both "speech" and "the thing spoken of."

גָּדוֹל

While this word may look as though it has the form קָטָאל, its form is probably קָטֵל, and more properly belongs with words that have the Biblical form קָטֹל:

אָרֹךְ	long		
גָּבֹהַּ	high	עָמֹק	deep
קָרוֹב	near	רָחוֹק	far
נָכֹחַ	straight	יָגֹל	round
גָּדוֹל	big	קָטֹן	small
טָהוֹר	pure	קָדֹשׁ	holy
אָדֹם	red	יָרֹק	green
צָהֹב	yellow	צָחֹר	white

אוֹ דָּבָר קָטֹן

אוֹ, meaning *or*, has been called "the particle of choice." It goes back to a root אוה, meaning *to go towards, to be inclined to* or *to desire*. Thus the abstract notion of either/or seems to have first come to sight as a conflict of desires. Such etymologies are particularly interesting since we might easily have taken the word *or* as a simple, readily-available concept rather than recognizing it to be the outcome of an archaic process of thinking.

וְלֹא יִגְלֶה

The root גלי means *to uncover* and is related to the root גלל, meaning *to be rolled up*. Here again we have an instance of opposite meanings living within the same cluster. It should also be noted here that Hebrew has no question mark.

אֶת־אָזְנִי

אֹזֶן, from the form קֶטֶל, means *ear*. The verbal form, *to listen*, has a rather poetic feeling to it—something like our "to give ear." That might suggest that in this case the nominal form is prior to the verbal. If that is so, it could be a sign that אֹזֶן is related to a Coptic word for *a peak*. Other words having this form include:

אֹזֶן	ear	גֹּבַהּ	height
עֹרֶף	neck	עֹמֶק	depth
בֹּהֶן	thumb	אֹרֶךְ	length
אֹהֶל	tent	רֹחַב	width
		גֹּדֶל	bigness/size

וּמַדּוּעַ

Note that when the ו connective precedes one of the other labials, ב, מ or פ—or any letter pronounced in the *shewa* mode—it becomes *shuruk* (וּ). If, however, the letter pronounced in the shewa mode is a י, the ו is pointed with a *hireq*, as in וִיהוּדָה.

The word מַדּוּעַ means *why*; but it must be distinguished from the word לָמָה, which means literally *to what*. The question לָמָה asks for the final cause; in other words, it asks the question *why* in the sense of wanting to know the ends or purposes of a given state or action. The question מַדּוּעַ, on the other hand, tends more to ask what prior condition gave rise to the present circumstances. Some scholars think that מַדּוּעַ comes from the words מָה + יָדוּעַ, that is, a combination of *what + is known*. But it is equally probable that the מ is from the word מִן, meaning *from*.

יַסְתִּיר

The reader can probably guess that the word יַסְתִּיר is some kind of third person singular in the hollow form of the root סתר; but the second י is somewhat confusing. If we look at the solid form, however, its derivation becomes clearer. The masculine third person singular is הִסְתִּיר and the first person is הִסְתַּרְתִּי. The first *hireq* is simply due to the law of lightening, but the ה itself is more interesting. It is a shred of the word הוּא, and thus we seem here to be dealing with a third way in which pronouns can attach themselves to roots.

We shall begin our explanation of this way by constructing the full range of possibilities, but this is not to imply that all of the possible forms actually exist in the language. On the contrary, many of them may never have existed. Some of them probably existed once but have been lost; and others, while still existing in the language, have altered their meanings, and moreover many vocalic shifts have taken place. For the present we shall consider only the masculine third person singular of the solid form; and we shall suppose that each pronoun can combine with either the simple level or with the forceful one.[1]

The three new sets of forms we shall call, respectively, the first, second, and third *constructions* (בִּנְיָנִים). The term *construction* (literally, *building*) is a traditional term in Hebrew grammar; but the reader should be aware of the fact that I am not using it in its time-honored sense, since traditional grammar does not make a radical distinction between constructions and levels.

Theoretical Schema of the Three Constructions

	Ground	1st construction	2nd construction	3rd construction
Simple	קָטַל	נִקְטַל	אֶתְקָטַל	הֻקְטַל
Forceful	קַטֵּל	נִקַטֵּל	אֶתְקַטֵּל	הֻקְטַל

When the first person pronoun joins itself to the root in this manner to form the first construction, it implies reflexivity. The kinship between the first person and the reflexive should by no means be strange to speakers of English. Although we often say *himself* and *themselves*, the word *self*, by itself, primarily means the I, the first person. This kinship also makes sense from a more universal point of view because in reflexivity the subject faces the object as a first person, as in a mirror.

---

1. Not all the Semitic languages have such a simple schema. Arabic, for instance, has a good many more constructions than Hebrew does. However, in different ways those constructions too seem to have their roots in the pronouns.

There is no good English word to convey the sense of the second construction, though we often use the word "reflexive" for it as well. Its sense, however, is perhaps better caught by our phrase *each other*. The relationship between this kind of reflexivity (which might better be called *reciprocality* or *mutuality*) and the second person is pretty clear: In mutuality each subject faces the other on equal terms as a "you."

The third construction is usually called the *causative*. It implies that the subject of the sentence does not do the act implied in the root but causes a third person to do it. English has no simple way of expressing the causative, but it accomplishes the same thing in a variety of ways. Sometimes one has only to choose a transitive rather than an intransitive verb, as when we say *I hide the treasure* rather than just *I hide*. When I hide the treasure, I cause the treasure to do what I do when I hide. Sometimes English uses a completely different verb to express the causative: *I came* is reflexive, but to express the causative we say *I brought*—that is, *I caused another to come.*

It occasionally happens that the ground form itself has a kind of causative meaning, such as the word שָׁלַח, which means *to send*. In these cases the third construction merely strengthens the notion. Thus the word הִשְׁלִיח does not mean *he caused to send* but *he hurled*.

It must be emphasized that there was a great deal of freedom and play involved as roots went from construction to construction. Consequently one cannot mechanically derive, from its ground meaning, the meaning which a root assumes in any of its constructed forms. However, some reflection will often make the means of transition clear.

Up to now in our theoretical treatment, we have supposed the vocalic mode of the first letter of the root to remain intact throughout all forms; but in fact it too has a role to play. The whole system as outlined above was reduplicated, only now with the first vowel becoming ֻ (*U-mode*). This alteration changed the verb from active to passive.

Let us therefore look again at the previous chart of the theoretical schema. If we exclude those forms which probably never existed and also take into account the law of lightening, we shall have the following diagram, incorporating both the active and the passive verb forms:

Actual Schema of the Three Constructions

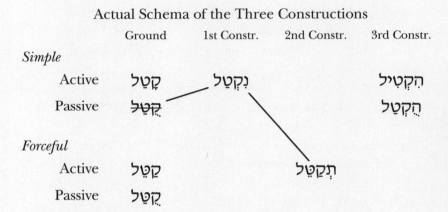

	Ground	1st Constr.	2nd Constr.	3rd Constr.
Simple				
Active	קָטַל	נִקְטַל		הִקְטִיל
Passive	קֻטַּל			הֻקְטַל
Forceful				
Active	קַטֵּל		תְקַטֵּל	
Passive	קֻטַּל			

As the system evolved, several additional changes took place. Because of the law of lightening, קַטִּטַל קַטַל or קָטְטַל became קְטַטֵּל or קְטֵל. People then began to hear the *I*-mode sound as part of the forcefulness of the form and no longer distinguished between קַטֵל and קֻטַל. Consequently, the form קֻטַל was all but completely dropped from the language. This left the simple form without a passive, although one can still occasionally find a קָטֻל whose dictionary meaning is the passive of the simple form.

In order to fill that gap, the form נִקְטַל came to be used as the passive of the simple form, its normal force in Biblical Hebrew. For example, לָכַד means *to capture*, but נִלְכַּד means *he was captured* rather than *he captured himself*. Nonetheless, one often finds נִקְטַל verbs still used in the old sense. For example, the verb כָּנַסְתִּי means *to collect* or *gather*, but the verb נִכְנַסְתִּי means *I entered*, that is, *I gathered myself* (into the room).

Often, then, the הִתְקַטֵּל form took over the old role of the נִקְטַל, while keeping its own function as well; for example, מָכַר, *he sold*, and הִתְמַכֵּר, *he sold himself.* Note also that under the influence of the third construction, the form אֶתְקַטֵּל became הִתְקַטֵּל, though it still retains the form אֶתְקַטֵּל in many other Semitic languages.

Since we began this note by considering the word יַסְתִּיר we should mention that it means *to hide something.* The verb does not exist in the ground form, but in the first construction it means *to hide oneself.*

The traditional names of these forms are:

Traditional Names of the Grammatical Forms

	Ground	1st Constr.	2nd Constr.	3rd Constr.
Simple				
Active	קַל	נִפְעַל		הִפְעִיל
Passive				הָפְעַל
Forceful				
Active	פִּעֵל		הִתְפָּעֵל	
Passive	פֻּעַל			

אָבִי מִמֶּנִּי אֶת־הַדָּבָר הַזֶּה

The word זֶה means *this*. The feminine form is זֹאת and the plural is אֵלֶּה. The situation appears to be quite disorderly or even hopeless, since the plural has no etymological connection to the singular. The following explanation, though lengthy, may help.

We must begin by looking at the situation as it appears in Akkadian and Arabic. Both these languages distinguish between the "near" and the "far" demonstrative—between "this" and "that," as listed in the following charts:

"This"

	Akkadian	*Arabic*
masc. sing.	אַנּוּ	(הָא)דָא*
fem. sing.	אַנִּיתֶ	(הָא)דְה
masc. plur.	אַנּוּתֶ	(הָא)אֶלָא
fem. plur.	אַנָּאתֶ	

* Note that in Arabic, as differentiated from Hebrew, ד and ד are two entirely separate letters, each standing on its own. In fact, to judge by cognates, Arabic ד was felt to be more akin to ז than it was to ד. Similarly, פ and כ are two separate letters in Arabic.

"That"

	Akkadian	*Arabic*
masc. sing.	אַלּוּ	דָאלְךָ
fem. sing.	אַלִּיתֶ	תִלְךָ
masc. plur.	אַלּוּתֶ	אֶלָאךְ
fem. plur.	אַלָּאתֶ	

The first thing to note is that Arabic words containing the letter דּ usually have Hebrew cognates spelled with a זּ; thus the Hebrew and Arabic words for *this* are cognate: compare Arabic הָאדָא with Hebrew הַזֶּה. On the other hand, the Arabic word for *that*, דָּאלְכָּ, corresponds to Hebrew זֶה לְךָ, which would bear the literal meaning "your this."

We also note that in Akkadian, the אל form appears only in the "far" case of the demonstrative. Thus it would seem that Hebrew uses the "near" form for the singular *this*, but the "far" form for the plural. In other words, while the dictionary meaning is *these*, the etymological meaning is *those*. Thus the notion of manyness has been conveyed by farness; or one might say that *greatness in number* was expressed by *greatness in distance*.

This argument has been rather lengthy, but it does restore a sense of order to the language. It might be worth noticing that the Akkadian "near" form is based on the נ (which rings of the first person) while the "far" form is based on אל. The Arabic דָּאלְכָּ suggests that the Akkadian "far" form also has the notion of *to* behind it.

אֵין זֹאת

אֵין is the leaning form of the noun אַיִן. That word means something like *nothingness*; When Job says יְקַו־לְאוֹר וָאַיִן, *Let it hope for light—and nothingness* (Job 3:9), one can feel the sudden cold emptiness of a nothingness. The same is true of the verse וְאָדָם אַיִן לַעֲבֹד אֶת־הָאֲדָמָה—*And of mankind, there was none to till the ground* (Genesis 2:6).

The leaning form is used for negation of nouns generally, and in particular for actor nouns (participles). In the following verse the noun אִישׁ is negated: וְאִישׁ אֵין בָּאָרֶץ—*and there is not a man in the earth* (Genesis 19:31). The participle הֹלְכִים is negated in the verse אִם־אֵין פָּנֶיךָ הֹלְכִים אַל־תַּעֲלֵנוּ מִזֶּה—*If your presence does not go [with us], carry us not from here.* (Exodus 33:15).[2]

---

2. Note that the plural הֹלְכִים is used here in order to agree with פָּנֶיךָ, which is itself plural because it is the leaning form of the plural פָּנִים (see page 73 above), here leaning upon the second person singular ending.

Finally, אֵין may also take personal endings, as in the phrase אֵינֶנִּי נֹתֵן לָכֶם—*I will not give to you* (Exodus 5:10). The expression literally means "my non-being gives you."

The leaning form does not always lean on the word that follows directly after it. An example is אֵין לָהּ וָלָד—*And there was not to her a child* (Genesis 11:30)—where אֵין actually leans on the word וָלָד.

Some scholars seem to believe that the word goes back to the Hebrew root איה, meaning *where*. Although I am not fully persuaded by the argument, if such is in fact the case, we may have an answer to questions raised previously concerning the word לא. This time it appears as though negativity came neither from malaise nor from a general feeling of lack in the universe, but from a definite search for a definite missing object. The question *Where is...?*, as in the question, *Where are the snows of yesteryear?*, always implies a kind of having of what one does not have. An articulated question seems to suggest a looking for a specifically known *this*, rather then a simple staring into nothingness. If such is the case, one would have to reconsider the suggestion made by some scholars that לא comes from ל. Rather, negativity would again have arisen out of directedness, inasmuch as it would be given by the word *to* plus the old accusative ending.

When לא is used with a noun it has a much greater force than does אֵין. When Amos says to Amaziahu לֹא נָבִיא אָנֹכִי, *I am not a prophet* (Amos 7:14), he is neither reporting nor lamenting, but forcefully rejecting the notion.

I would suggest that לא has its roots in the act of rejection, whereas אֵין has behind it a feeling of loss or of emptiness.

12. I Samuel 20:3

וַיִּשָּׁבַע עוֹד דָּוִד וַיֹּאמֶר יָדֹעַ יָדַע כִּי־מָצָאתִי חֵן 3
בְּעֵינֶיךָ וַיֹּאמֶר אַל־יֵדַע־זֹאת יְהוֹנָתָן פֶּן־יֵעָצֵב וְאוּלָם
חַי־יְהוָֹה וְחֵי נַפְשֶׁךָ כִּי כְפֶשַׂע בֵּינִי וּבֵין הַמָּוֶת:

Notes on the reading:

וַיִּשָּׁבַע

The root שׁבע means *to swear*. It may or may not be related to
the word שֶׁבַע which means *seven*. It has been suggested that the
original meaning was *I seven myself*, or *I bind myself by seven things*.
The fact that the number seven has always had a certain aura
about it makes this suggestion quite plausible. On the other hand
it must always be kept in mind the same forces that allow for the
growth of the clusters often lead to accidental mergers.

עוֹד דָּוִד

עוֹד, which means *again* or *yet*, is one of the few apparent
adverbs in the Hebrew language. It comes from the root עוד,
meaning *to return* or *to repeat*.

וַיֹּאמֶר יָדֹעַ יָדַע

The word יָדֹעַ, which has the form קָטֹל with the patah added
to assist the ע, comes from an original form קָטָאל. The original
form should be thought of as being on a par with the forms קָטַל
and קָטֵל, which formed the bases of the solid and hollow states,
respectively. This קָטֹל form, which might be called the *supersolid*
state, implies a sense of certainty beyond that of the solid state;
but unlike both the solid and the hollow states, it retained its
independence and never conjoined itself to the pronouns. It
simply refers to the activity itself and is generally referred to as the
infinite absolute. We may look upon it as a kind of living dinosaur,
as its use—directed purely towards the activity itself without any

95

modification by a *who* or a *when*—appears to give us a glimpse
into an archaic world.

In Biblical Hebrew its force is closely connected to what is
called the *cognate accusative*. We often use this form in English in
expressions such as *he danced a dance, he sang a song,* or *he thought a
thought*. To understand this better, consider the distinction
between the sentences *he danced a dance* and *he danced a jig*. The
jig is a formalized dance composed of certain well-known steps. In
that sense it exists apart from any particular act of dancing. If, on
the other hand, we say *he danced a dance*, we refer to a dance that
exists only while it is going on. Similarly, if someone makes a
table, the table continues to exist apart from its maker; someone
else can happen along and use it. But if a someone dances a
dance, the dance ceases to exist when the dancing ceases. The
dance is then not a product but an activity. In that sense, the
cognate accusative tends to strengthen the verb; and in Hebrew it
often does no more than that. Generally speaking, the form is not
very common in Hebrew, though we will meet quite a few
instances of it in this particular passage.

The root יָדַע, which once meant *to observe*, here means *to know*;
and the whole phrase יָדֹעַ יָדַע may be translated as *knowing, he
knew*, or *he surely knew*.

אָבִיךָ כִּי־מָצָאתִי

The word מָצָאתִי, from the root מצא, is weak because of the א
in the third position. The major vocalic changes are due to the
propensity of the א to become vocalic, and they are as follows:

$$מָצָאתָ ← מָצָאתָ$$
$$יִמְצָא ← יִמְצָא$$
$$נִמְצָאתִי ← מָצֵאתִי$$

Note that if strictly pronounced, a syllable ending in א would end
in a glottal stop (compare the first syllable of the English negative
grunt *uh'uh*.) Hebrew, however, tends to avoid this. In general,
there are two ways to deal with a final א. One way is to take the א
as a consonantal vowel; in the present example that would have
led to the form מְצָאתָ. The second way is what actually happens
in this case: the א is simply ignored, and the syllable is treated as if
it were an open syllable. But the א is retained in writing since it is
a definitive letter of the root.

Very much the same thing happens in the hollow state, but in the first construction (see page 88) the pattern follows the example of the forceful level, where קָטַל became קָטֵל.

The root מצא means *to find* or *to meet*, whether by chance or by intent.

חֵן

חֵן, meaning grace, comes from the root חנן which originally meant extreme feelings of either joy or grief.

בְּעֵינֶיךָ

עַיִן originally meant *eye* and is closely connected to the verb עין, which means *to look at*. In that sense it is like the word אֹזֶן (ear), which we came upon earlier. Similarly, the word for *foot*, רֶגֶל, is related to the word *to sneak* or *to spy*, and the word for *nose* is related to the verb *to blow*; it is as if we were to speak of the parts of the body as *the listeners, the lookers, the blower, the sneakers,* and (in the case of the fingers) *the pointers*. In English, we too have such expressions as *to eye* something. While in English it is clear in all such cases that the name for the activity comes from the noun, in Hebrew the situation is less clear and may indicate an original unity.

וַיֹּאמֶר אַל־יֵדַע־זֹאת יְהוֹנָתָן פֶּן־יֵעָצֵב

פֶּן, which is normally translated *lest*, comes from the root פנה, which we have seen before in the word פָּנִים. The original notion in the root was *turn* in the double sense of either *turning to* or *turning from*. From this latter sense it came to mean *Turn from…!* or *Let it not…!*

יֵעָצֵב

יֵעָצֵב is the first construction from the root עצב. Its form is יִקָּטֵל. The full paradigm is shown in Chart 12.1 on the following page. Note there that in the hollow state the נ of the first construction has been devoured by the ק, but its echo is present as the dagesh in the ק; thus יִנְקָטֵל became יִקָּטֵל. The need to preserve the נ in this way was felt so strongly that, in the imperative, a ה was added because no syllable can begin with a doubling dagesh.

As was mentioned earlier, at some point there was a shift in the significance of the first construction, and in the text one can find

First Construction (נִפְעַל)

HOLLOW		SOLID		
plural	*singular*	*plural*	*singular*	
יִקָּטְלוּ	יִקָּטֵל	נִקְטְלוּ	נִקְטַל	3rd masc.
תִּקָּטֵלְנָה	תִּקָּטֵל	נִקְטְלוּ	נִקְטְלָה	3rd fem.
תִּקָּטְלוּ	תִּקָּטֵל	נִקְטַלְתֶּם	נִקְטַלְתָּ	2nd masc.
תִּקָּטֵלְנָה	תִּקָּטְלִי	נִקְטַלְתֶּן	נִקְטַלְתְּ	2nd fem.
נִקָּטֵל	אֶקָּטֵל	נִקְטַלְנוּ	נִקְטַלְתִּי	1st c.

plural		*singular*		
fem.	masc.	fem.	masc.	
הִקָּטֵלְנָה	הִקָּטְלוּ	הִקָּטְלִי	הִקָּטֵל	Imperative
נִקְטָלֹת	נִקְטָלִים	נִקְטָלָה	נִקְטָל	Participle

Infinitive
(לְ)הִקָּטֵל

Chart 12.1.

many examples of both the old and the new. Originally, the first construction had a reflexive intent. For example, the root סְפח means *to join or attach*; but the word נספח does not mean *to be joined*, but rather *to join up with*. On the other hand, גזר means *to cut off*, while נגזר means *to be cut off*.

The root עצב is weak in that the first root letter is guttural. Since the letter ע cannot accept a dagesh, we have יֵעָצֵב instead of יֵעָצֵב.

The Semitic root עצב originally meant *to strike*, or *to make powerless*; in the first construction it means *to be grieved*; in this case one can feel the kinship between the reflexive and the passive.

וְאוּלָם

אוּלָם, which more or less means *but*, comes from a root meaning *to bind* in the sense of *putting restraints upon*, and eventually comes to mean *speechless* or *dumb*. As we have seen, the

U-mode in the first position is the mark of the passive. It is not so difficult to see a *but* phrase as indicating a fettered thought.

חַי־יהוה

חַי is the leaning form of the word חַיִּים meaning *animate life*. The word חַיָּה, which means *animal*, is never used for barnyard creatures but only for those who live in the fields, and all the more if they are wild or dangerous. Closely connected to that wild and dangerous aspect of the word is the fact that the word חַיִּים, or *life,* exists only in the plural.

The second word in this phrase, יהוה, is the name of God, the word that is sometimes transliterated Jehovah. Traditionally it is considered too holy to pronounce, and observant Jews substitute words like אֲדוֹנָי (*Lord*) or הַשֵּׁם (*The Name*) instead. In fact the vocalic modes of יהוה are unknown and its correct pronunciation not recorded. By tradition it was only to be spoken by the High Priest and only in the Holy of Holies, when the Temple stood. Since then the pronunciation has been lost.

וְחֵי נַפְשְׁךָ כִּי כְפֶשַׂע

The word פֶּשַׂע means *step,* and it seems to go back to the more concrete Akkadian word for *foot.*

בֵּינִי וּבֵין הַמָּוֶת

The root בין is weak. Note that in both בֵּינִי and וּבֵין the root letter י has become a consonantal vowel. We shall consider this kind of root in greater detail the next time it appears in a verbal form.

The root in Akkadian means *to be distinct,* and in Hebrew it exists in the third construction where it means *to cause to be distinct* or *to view as being distinct.* As is often the case with words in the third construction, the sense of causation refers to something that happens in thought alone; thus the word הֵבִין means *to cause to be distinct in thought,* that is, *to understand.* A similar example is the word הִצְדִּיק, *to consider a thing to be just,* from the root צדק, *to be just.*

When the prepositions came to be, the phrase "A divides B from C" came to be heard as "A is between B and C." Thus, בין became the Hebrew word for *between.*

13. I Samuel 20:4
What is a Verse?

4 וַיֹּ֙אמֶר֙ יְהֽוֹנָתָ֖ן אֶל־דָּוִ֑ד מַה־תֹּאמַ֥ר נַפְשְׁךָ֖ וְאֶעֱשֶׂה־לָּֽךְ׃

By now you should be able to translate the whole of this verse without any help from the author. You might, however, be confused by the last word, which seems either to be of the wrong gender or to have undergone a shift in its vocalic mode. In fact, the latter has happened. To understand that shift, we shall have to make a new beginning.

The first chapters of this book dealt with the sounds and letters of the Hebrew language. Subsequent chapters dealt with the ways in which those sounds came together to form words. But we have yet to deal in any coherent fashion with the ways in which words come together to form meaningful sentences.

If you have been following the pointed text you may have noticed that each word has one of several marks we have not yet considered. These marks are called *ta'amim* (singular: *ta'am*). There is no common agreement among scholars as to the primary meanings of the ta'amim. With very few exceptions, each one clearly marks the accented syllable. However, they have two other functions: they are both grammatical and musical, and although these two elements are intimately connected, it is not clear whether the inventors had grammar or music in mind when they first established the ta'amim. If the ta'amim are musical, they must differ greatly from even the earliest neumes[1] of Gregorian chant. From the very beginning, the shapes of the neumes obviously represented changes of pitch written for a particular passage of text and could not be confused with grammar: when the musical notes went up, the pitch went up; and when the notes fell, the pitch fell. Nothing quite so simple is true of our ta'amim. In the following paragraphs we shall not try to resolve whether the ta'amim are primarily musical or primarily grammatical, but merely try to understand how such a question is possible.

---

1. Neumes were elements of medieval musical notation. A single neume might represent a single note, a sequence of two or three notes, or even a short melodic "tunelet."

Our account will cover the notational system as it appears in the so-called prose books of the Bible. The so-called poetical books—*Psalms, Proverbs* and *The Book of Job*—work according to a different system, which we have not included in our treatment.

Let us begin by looking at the ta'amim as music. But what can it mean to *look* at music? Music is, after all, meant to be heard and not seen. Perhaps, though, there is an answer. Suppose you are a serious, but untrained, musical listener. If you were to pick up a musical score you might ask yourself whether you could find any order in the written symbols that might reflect at least some of the characteristics you had heard in the music. You would first notice rather simple things, such as that in simple tunes the vertical spacing between successive notes tends to be small, usually no more than a full step between successive notes. You might also begin to notice that certain groups of notes are repeated, sometimes simply and sometimes with variation. Sometimes the note patterns are even turned upside-down as if in answer to an earlier succession of notes. Perhaps you would notice too that long phrases tend to end on one particular note, and that other notes tend to come before it as if to prepare the way. Let us try to look at our passage with such an eye[2] to see what order, if any, emerges among the ta'amim in the text.

Having committed ourselves to investigating the ta'amim from a purely musical point of view, we must forget about speech. Since the ta'amim appear sometimes above the words and sometimes below them, we shall place them that way upon the page and look only at the ta'amim themselves. Remember to read them from right to left! Our verse would then transform like this:

וַיֹּאמֶר יְהוֹנָתָן אֶל־דָּוִד מַה־תֹּאמַר נַפְשְׁךָ וְאֶעֱשֶׂה־לָּךְ׃

The secret of such investigations is to be as naive as possible and not to fear spelling out the obvious. The pattern above appears rather simple. All of the ta'amim are on the bottom, and the final mark is simply a straight line (ˌ), as if to stop the whole. In the middle there is a mark that rather resembles a fulcrum (˄), and it is surrounded by two sets resembling the lower halves of parentheses (ˎ and ˏ). Let us now rewrite the first four verses of I Samuel 20 in this same way:

---

2. Levi-Strauss describes a similarly fanciful approach to deciphering musical notation. See his *Structural Anthropology*, p. 212.

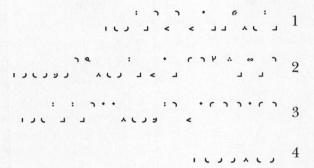

From these four examples, several new things come to light. Each of the four verses still ends with a vertical line and each has one and only one fulcrum, but the fulcrum is not necessarily in the geographical center of the sentence.

The remaining ta'amim—dots, half-parentheses, and others—appear to fall into two families: *superscripts* written exclusively above the line, and *subscripts* placed exclusively below it. With two exceptions, the superscripts tend to cluster together, while the subscripts tend form two separate groups, one ending at the fulcrum, the other at the end of the verse. The two exceptions are the subscripts ⌐ and ⌐, which, though written below the line, are scattered so freely throughout the superscripts, it is almost as if they belonged to both families. Both of these ta'amim, moreover, seem to draw our eye forward.

Having noted these things, let us render the ta'am pattern of the first twelve verses of I Samuel 20 twice. The first time we include all the ta'amim:

Now writing a second time we leave out the two ta'amim in question, obtaining:

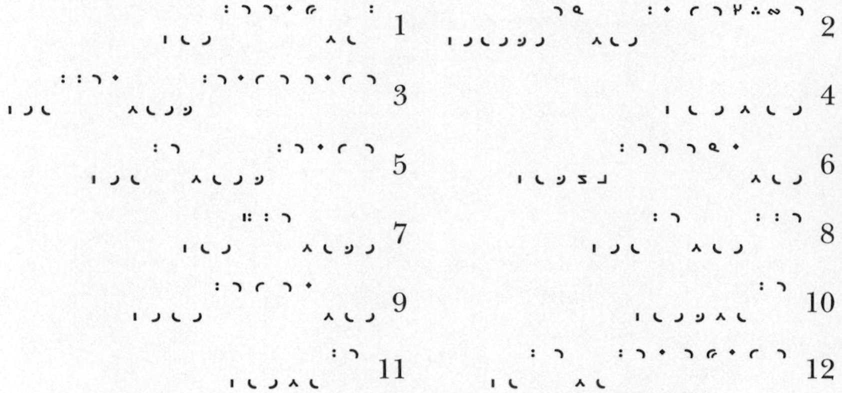

Rewritten in this second way, additional bits of order begin to reveal themselves. First, the ta'amim generally begin above the line but drop below it as they approach the fulcrum ; after the fulcrum they may appear above the text again, but they drop back below it as they approach the end of the verse.[3]

If we consider the final ta'am, , we see that it can appear in the following contexts:

If we momentarily consider the ta'amim as if they were parentheses, we might sum up the possibilities this way.

The final ta'am concludes the whole. It can act as if it closed a set of parentheses: . It can be preceded (though not necessarily immediately) by a closed pair of parentheses: ; and this pair may itself be preceded by a dotted opening parenthesis: .

The draws the eye backward, and thereby seems to hold its word back a bit from what follows, as in the pattern . By contrast, the in either of the patterns or seems rather to hold two words together, giving more or less equal weight to both. The pattern in verse 7 represents another way to hold two words together; but instead of showing equality, the first word here seems to lean on, or lead into, the second, while the second seems to stand more on its own.

3. Exception: If the portion either before or after the fulcrum is short, as in verses 4, 6, or 11 above, the ta'amim in that portion may begin below rather than above the line.

Note that the only ⌣ in the text is preceded by the only ⌢. Such observations suggest dividing the signs into several groups. The names of these groups, and of the ta'amim that belong to them, are:[4]

MAJOR STOPS

1.	׀	סִלּוּק	Silluq	"Cessation"
2.	֑	אַתְנָח	Athnah	"Cause to rest"
3.	֖	סְגוֹלְתָּא	S'golta	"Halting"
4.	֒	זָקֵף	Zaqeph	"Raising up"
5.	֗	רְבִיעַ	R'bhia	"Resting"

MINOR or SEQUENTIAL STOPS

6.	֖	טִפְחָא	Tiphha	"Thrusting back"
7.	֘	זַרְקָא	Zarqa	"Scatter"
8.	֙	פַּשְׁטָא	Pashta	"Extended"
9.	֜	גֶּרֶשׁ	Geresh	"Expulsion"
10.	֓	תְּבִיר	T'bhir	"Broken"
11.	֒	תְּלִישָׁא גְדוֹלָא	T'lisha g'dola (great t'lisha)	"Great drawn-out"
12.	֞	פָּזֵר	Pazer	"Diffuse"

CONNNECTIVES

13.	֥	מֵירְכָא	Merkha	"Prolonged"
14.	֓	מוּנַח	Munah	"Sustained"
15.	֧	דַרְגָּא	Darga	"A step"
16.	֤	מְהֻפָּךְ	M'huppakh	"Inverted"
17.	֝	אַזְלָא	Azla	"Ongoing"
18.	֑	תְּלִישָׁא קְטַנָּא	T'lisha q'tannah (lesser t'lisha)	"Small drawn-out"
19.	֪	גַּלְגַּל	Galgal	"A wheel"

---

4. The names of some of the ta'amim differ in different traditions. I am using the names generally adopted by grammarians.

Although azla and pashta are identical in shape, they can be distinguished from one another by context, as we shall see. Additional ta'amim will appear later under special circumstances, but the foregoing chart will suffice for an initial presentation.[5] Thus far, then, we can understand the musical structure of a verse in terms of the following principles:

(1) Each verse ends with a silluq and has one athnah, as

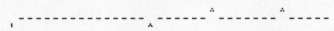

Note that since almost every verse has an athnah, it is not possible to speak of its absolute value as one might, say, of a semicolon. In that way the ta'amim are not comparable to western punctuation marks. It would be better instead to think of the athnah as marking, so to speak, the center of gravity of the sentence; the athnah is said to divide each verse into two more or less equal *versets*. If the first verset is sufficiently complicated, it may then be broken up into as many *divisions* as necessary, these breaks being indicated by s'goltas. In the following example, the first verset is broken up into three divisions:

(2) The second verset may be divided directly—and the divisions of the first verset may be further subdivided—by the zaqeph, like this:

While the s'golta is used sparingly before the athnah, it never occurs after it. This would suggest that the rhetoric of the biblical language is such that the first verset tends to be more complex than the second verset.

(3) Finally, divisions made by the zaqeph may be further divided by the r'bhia, as here:

---

5. Zarqa, s'golta, and the lesser t'lisha are always written on the final syllable, even if the final syllable is not the accented one. In the latter case a duplicate zarqa, s'golta, or lesser t'lisha is placed on the accented syllable.

As indicated in the chart on page 105, all the foregoing ta'amim—silluq, athnah, s'golta, zaqeph, and r'bhia—are *major stops*. The silluq ends the entire verse, the athnah marks its center of gravity, the s'golta, zaqeph, and r'bhia divide it into finer and finer portions. Further subdivisions, if needed, are made in a somewhat different spirit: each of the major stops is approached by its own proper sequence of *minor* or *sequential* stops, as shown in the following chart. If only one sequential stop is needed, the last in the sequence is used; if two, then the last two, and so on:

THE MAJOR STOPS AND THE
SEQUENTIAL STOPS LEADING UP TO THEM

1.	2.	3.	4.	5.
ז פ ע	ז פ ע	∴ ש ז פ ע	ֹ ז פ ע	• ר פ ע
ן ל ֶ	∧ ל ֶ			

Note that the sequences leading up to subscripts silluq (ֽ) and athnah (֑) are identical. The sequences preceding superscripts s'golta (֝), zaqeph (֔), and r'bhia (֗) are almost identical, but the r'bhia takes a geresh (֜) instead of a pashta (֙) as its immediate predecessor, and the sequence leading up to s'golta includes the zarqa, thereby permitting one additional division. This reflects the fact that divisions made by s'golta tend to be longer and more complicated than those made by zaqeph or r'bhia. As to *why* the r'bhia takes geresh rather than pashta, however, I have little to offer. I suspect, though, that the answer lies in the musical chant, insofar as one pattern is musically more intricate than the other.[6]

To illustrate the order of sequential stops, consider a division that is made by s'golta, then further subdivided by a zaqeph:

Now the chart above dictates that if there is only one sequential stop before the s'golta, it must be zarqa; we shall have:

If there are two sequential stops, the zarqa will be preceded by pashta:

---

6. Traditions disagree, however, as to whether geresh or pashta takes the more intricate chant pattern.

And if there are three sequential stops, the pashta will be preceded by a greater t'lisha:

$$\underset{\cdot\cdot}{}\ \text{- - -}\ \overset{\sim}{\text{- - -}}\ \overset{)}{}\ \ \text{- - -}\ \overset{\circ}{\text{- - -}}\ \overset{:}{}\ \text{- - - - - - -}$$

In general, once a sequence of sequential stops has begun, it must culminate in its own proper major stop before another sequence can commence.

Up to this point we have considered these major stops:

Silluq ( ), which divides verse from verse

Athnah ( ), which divides a verse into two versets

S'golta ( ), Zaqeph ( ), and R'bhia ( ), which
mark further subdivisions

We have also considered the following minor, or sequential, stops:

Tiphha ( ), Zarqa ( ), Pashta ( ), Geresh ( ),

T'bhir ( ), T'lisha g'dola ( ), and Pazer ( ).

Between these stops lies the text—or, to speak more precisely, every stop, whether major or sequential, ends what we shall call a *phrase*; the next word begins a new phrase, and so the text is composed of phrases. The inner structure of each phrase is held together by a sequence of ta'amim that I call *connectives*.

Every word receives a ta'am indicating the role it plays in the structure of the verse. Rather like our sentence diagrams, then, the ta'amim contain an implicit understanding of grammar. They show the general structure of each verse by marking its parts, beginning with the athnah and working down to the level of the sequential stops. The words we find in the biblical text then present themselves as being ordered into phrases as connective sequences; the stops indicate how these phrases come together to form greater and greater wholes. The early Hebrew grammarians acknowledged this hierarchical structure by calling the stops "emperors," "kings," and "dukes," while the connectives they called "servants." Since in actual verses the context may become rather complicated we will only be able to offer examples of some of the simplest connective sequences.

As was the case with the sequential stops, the connectives display an order of precedence. In the following chart, if only one connective is required the one closest to the stop is used; while if the phrase is more complex, it may be held together in one of the following ways:

CONSTRUCTION OF SEQUENCES

Sequences Ending in Major Stops

1.   2.   3.   4.   5.

Sequences Ending in Sequential Stops

6.   7.   8.   9.   10.

11.   12.

In order to see how the major stops, sequential stops, and connectives relate to one another, let us look at the music of the following verse. It is a rather long passage and will provide us ample opportunity to see a wide range of relations:

To begin, then, let us consider only the major and the sequential stops; this will give the basic outline of the music. Our first step will be to rewrite the verse with the connectives omitted.[7] For convenience, we have numbered individual divisions.

8	7	6	5	4	3	2	1

The first division (1) contains only the r'bhia; the second division (2) ends in s'golta approached by one sequential stop, a zarqa. The third division (3) ends in zaqeph approached by one sequential stop, a pashta. Division (4) ends with athnaḥ approached the sequential stop tiphḥa. Division (5) ends in zaqeph approached by pashta, just as in (3).

Division (6) ends in r'bhia approached by the full set of sequential stops indicated in sequence 4 of the chart on page 107. Division (7) ends in zaqeph approached by two sequential stops, t'lisha g'dola and pashta. The last division (8) ends with silluq approached by two sequential stops, t'bhir and tiphḥa.

This still leaves many musically unordered words. Connectives were therefore appointed to them according to the chart above

---

7. Since azla (conjoining motif) and pashta (major stop) resemble one another, some experience is required to identify the motifs. Later in our discussion you will be able to see how the context serves to facilitate this identification.

showing Construction of Sequences. Let us therefore write the verse again, this time restoring the connectives and distinguishing some of the individual phrases:

$$\underset{13}{}\ \underset{12}{}\ \underset{11}{}\ \underset{10}{}\ \underset{9}{}\ \underset{8}{}\ \underset{7}{}\ \underset{6}{}\ \underset{5}{}\ \underset{4}{}\ \underset{3}{}\ \underset{2}{}\ \underset{1}{}$$

We recognize phrase (1) as sequence 5 in the chart on page 109, and phrase (2) as sequence 7. Phrase (3) is just the s'golta itself. In phrase (4) and again in (8) we see azla and m'huppakh leading up to pashta as in sequence 8. In phrase (5), munaḥ leading to zaqeph is sequence 4. The reader is invited to continue this analysis.

Lastly, consider phrases (10)–(13). Remembering that every word normally receives a single ta'am, we see that each is a one-word phrase except for (11), which has two words and therefore employs a single connective. But in order to see a more complex form, consider a verse with the same number of stops but which has a geater number of words in each connective sequence. Such a verse would require additional connectives, so that the phrases might come to look, for example, like this:

$$\underset{13}{}\ \underset{12}{}\ \underset{11}{}\ \underset{10}{}$$

Here phrase (10), which formerly consisted of only one word, now has three, the two words preceding the pazer having a munaḥ each (there are Biblical verses in which a pazer is preceded by as many as five words, each having a munaḥ). Phrase (12), which was also originally a single word, now contains four words. If the writer had instead employed only two words, there would have been no munaḥ and no lesser t'lisha.

Up to this point we have used the term *musical* in the most generic sense possible, but now we must say something about the music of Biblical verses, as music is commonly understood.

Even when looked at in terms of the chant, the ta'amim are not individual notes. In western music single tones become meaningful only in terms of the eight notes which form the scale. Those eight notes provide, as it were, a kind of Cartesian coordinate system in terms of which any given note assumes its proper character, just as a point has its own individual being only when it has its proper place on a Cartesian graph. Hebraic chant does not establish a scale but is, one might say, more Euclidean in nature. The smallest meaningful object is a given shape or, to use a more musical term, a given *trope* or *tunelet* that is represented by each of the ta'amim. These tropes then follow one another as cadences or as answers to questions according to the rules given above.

The specific trope assigned to each ta'am differs from country to country and from town to town in our day, but it may be possible from the ta'amim themselves to infer something about the general nature of the chant as it was originally conceived. As we noted before, the ta'amim generally begin above the line but drop permanently below the line as they approach the end of a verset; that is, as they approach either athnah or silluq. If we look back at the the twelve verse patterns on page 104, we can also see that except in the case of short verses, most of the chant goes on above the line, and that very few connectives are allowed once the drop has been made. If we suppose that the drop represents the distinction between high and low, as those terms are traditionally used in music, then it would seem that the chants represent a falling kind of music.

But what could the term *falling music* mean? Do not all tunes go up and down all the time? Consider western music as we have known and whistled it, since the time of Descartes and Monteverdi. As we sing the scale up and down, we can hear that the second note of the scale tends to pull us down to the first and that the seventh note tends to pull us up to the eighth; but we can also hear that the attraction of the seventh note to the eighth is much stronger than the tendency of the second note to fall back to the first. Rising music, music that culminates in the seventh note going to the eighth note of the scale, drives on to its goal. Falling music ends in relaxation. This distinction is also reflected in the fact that in western music we toy with false endings to prolong the cadence, whereas once the drop has been made in Hebraic chant, connectives are held to a minimum. This would imply that the chant is an ongoing activity which takes place above the line rather than a striving for a final goal.

But what great forces are brought into play to cause western music to rise so contrary to the laws of gravity? If you have a piano available, you can easily hear that the fourth and seventh notes of the scale, when struck together, are in disharmony; they produce a grating and unsettling sound. The seventh note, on the other hand, is only a half step from home. The striving character of western music was achieved by introducing this disharmony which is so close to, and so points towards, its conclusion. Falling music is an ongoing kind of music and rejects both the striving and the implied disharmony. What comes after the drop is a taking leave of the chant, rather then a buildup arriving at a culmination.

This would imply that the chant is an ongoing activity that takes place above the line, rather than a striving for a final goal. In line with this, most traditions agree that the stops tend to be associated with rather simple musical tropes, whereas the connectives tend to become quite intricate. In a synagogue service, however, the silluq of the final verse of the weekly Torah reading is usually treated more ornamentally than are other silluqim. In the West, silluq is almost always a falling trope—in some traditions it is a descending third, in others a descending fifth—but in the East it is usually a rising half tone.

Needless to say, it is not possible to infer anything about the musical tropes themselves from these appearances. Nevertheless, if we consider them with some care, it might be possible to make some reasonable conjecture concerning what in western terms would be called the dynamic relationships between the tropes. However, since Hebraic chant seems not to have had a striving character, perhaps the term *dynamic* does not quite apply. We might better simply speak of the way in which each trope lays the ground, or prepares the way, for the next.

The chant seems most fragile around the geresh (`). Every other mark leads to a specific conclusion, but the geresh is open to total ambiguity. It is not one of the major stops, and it therefore raises our expectations. Clear and familiar alternatives are before us, but we do not know which road the chant will take. The ambiguity has as wide a range as can possibly exist in Hebraic chant.

The geresh can be the precursor to the final drop foreshadowing the cessation of the chant by leading to a t'bhir (ˌ), or it can keep the chant going by remaining above the line. It can lead directly to a stop as in the case of the r'bhia, or it can lead to further sequential stops. More often, however, the geresh was deleted and is now present by implication only. It may have been heard, even if it was not actually sounded.

The first verset of Genesis 22:2, for example, reads:

Here the t'lisha ( ) should be followed by a geresh ( ), and the azla ( ) is geresh's proper connective; nevertheless the geresh itself does not appear. People may have heard it with an inner ear, but of course there is no way to know for sure.

Ambiguity must be handled with a great deal of care or it will lead to chaos. In the following paragraphs we shall try to outline some of the characteristics of the chant which make this ambiguity possible and yet keep it from falling into complete confusion. The musical area surrounding the geresh is always tricky, and many transformations must take place in order for the chant to maintain its character. We shall list nine of the many transformations that have been identified;[8] obviously we are only scratching the surface of this very elaborate topic. It should be noted that more care is needed to remain above the line than to allow the chant to relax and fall beneath it.

(1) The great t'lisha ( ), which clearly belongs to the upper realm, is not allowed to fall on the syllable preceding the word with the geresh.

(2) If the geresh falls near the beginning of a long word, it is replaced by a double geresh or *gershayim* ( ). Perhaps the quality of expectation had to be increased slightly in order to last through the intervening syllables—but that, of course, is no more than a guess.

(3) When the geresh is not preceded by its first connective, the azla ( ), it is also replaced by a gershayim. This might imply that the full ambiguity was contained only in the pair   .

(4) When the azla is not prepared for by a lesser t'lisha ( ), it tends to becomes simple munaḥ ( ).

(5) As we mentioned before, it is generally easier to drop after a geresh than to maintain the chant. Nonetheless, if there is a darga ( ) intervening between the geresh and the drop to the t'bhir ( ), and if the darga is less than two syllables away from the t'bhir, it becomes a merkha ( ). Presumably this is because the merkha has a stronger character of expectancy.

---

8. William Wickes, *Two Treatises on the Accentuation of the Old Testament* and S. Moscati et al., *An Introduction to the Comparative Grammar of the Semitic Languages.*

(6) The case of the pashta is similar. If its first connective, the m'huppakh (⸜) comes within one syllable of it, it too changes to a merkha.

(7) It would seem that the transition between the geresh and the pashta was not deemed sufficiently strong to allow one to rest above the line. At any rate, if there are no connectives between the pashta (⸜) and the zaqeph (⸐), the zaqeph had to be given a greater resting power. Thus it was changed into a great zaqeph (⸗).

(8) This weakness in the transition between the geresh and the pashta may also be seen by the fact that if the pashta is not preceded by a m'huppakh and falls on the first syllable of the word, it becomes a m'huppakh; that is, (⸜ ⸔) becomes (⸜ ⸜). Such a m'huppakh is called a yethibh. In some texts of the Bible the two signs are distinguished, and the yethibh is written as a small triangle; but as we shall see later, the ambiguity is probably not entirely accidental.

One other change may be related to maintaining the ambiguous character of the geresh. The s'golta (⸏) must be introduced by the zarqa (⸛); otherwise it becomes shalsheleth (⸰).

The new signs may be summarized as follows:

ADDITIONAL MAJOR STOPS

שַׁלְשֶׁלֶת	Shalsheleth	"Chain"
זָקֵף גָּדוֹל	Zaqeph gadol	Great Zaqeph

ADDITIONAL SEQUENTIAL STOPS

יְתִיב	Yethibh	"Pause"
גֵּרְשַׁיִם	Gershayim	Double Geresh

Now that we have begun to understand something of the chant, let us reconsider the first four verses of I Samuel 20. While the laws regulating the chant are simpler then those regulating western music, we still have some laws to pick up along the way. We will mention some of them as we meet the difficulties. Others you will face for yourself in your own reading. For a more complete account, refer to William Wickes' *Two Treatises on the Accentuation of the Old Testament*. Although Wickes' account is quite different from our own, his is a very carefully written book and should be quite helpful.

In order to facilitate the use of other grammar books, it should be mentioned that traditional grammars either do not distinguish between the major and the sequential stops, or do not understand that distinction to be as fundamental as I believe it to be. For that reason, most grammar books treat the r'bhia together with the pashta, rather then grouping it along with the other major stops.

You might want to try your hand at giving a complete account of the first four verses of I Samuel 20, but you will need a bit of help with the first one. The second verset of I Samuel 20:1 reads:

The difficulty lies in the passage that reads ⟨ ⟩. Let us first consider the sequence ⟨ ⟩. These ta'amim appear to be respectively azla, m'huppakh, and pashta—which makes sense since we know that the geresh may be suppressed. However, from the chart of Construction of Sequences on page 109 we know that an azla has as its predecessor a lesser t'lisha, so that the passage should have read ⟨ ⟩. But since the passage is actually written ⟨ ⟩, what seemed at first to be an azla must be a pashta instead. Normally, a sequence of two pashtas would be a fundamental error in the chant, for as we have seen, every sequence must culminate in one of the major stops before a new sequence can begin. This sequence, however, seems to begin with the m'huppakh, goes as far as the pashta, and then starts all over again. Such things rarely happen in chant; what has happened here may be stated as follows.

From the point of view of the grammar of the sentence, the first pashta should have been a r'bhia, and the passage should have read ⟨ ⟩. According to the laws of the chant, it is quite possible to culminate in a r'bhia, back off with a connective, then culminate again in a r'bhia without any higher culmination (such as a zarga or a s'golta) intervening. In our case, however, there is only one munah between the two culminations. This does not give the listener sufficient time to prepare for the second r'bhia. For this reason, the second r'bhia has been changed to a pashta. This is the kind of rule that the reader will have to pick up through practice along the way. Nevertheless, even after all of these rules are mastered, many difficulties will remain, the total number of which is great enough to force us to face a fundamental question concerning the chant. There seem to be only three possibilities. Either the manuscript tradition is extremely faulty with regard to the ta'amim, or a certain amount of freedom was allowed to the punctuator, or the present author has simply not discovered all of the laws. While I am aware of the importance of this question, by no means do I feel sufficiently competent to declare which is the case.

Let this suffice for our account of the musical interpretation of the ta'amim, and let us begin again from the beginning, this time looking at the ta'amim purely from the viewpoint of grammar. Recall verse 20:1, with which we began:

וַיִּבְרַ֣ח דָּוִ֔ד מִנָּיֹ֖ות בָּרָמָ֑ה וַיָּבֹ֣א וַיֹּ֣אמֶר ׀ לִפְנֵ֣י יְהֹונָתָ֗ן מֶ֤ה עָשִׂ֙יתִי֙ מֶֽה־עֲוֹנִ֤י וּמֶֽה־חַטָּאתִי֙ לִפְנֵ֣י אָבִ֔יךָ כִּ֥י מְבַקֵּ֖שׁ אֶת־נַפְשִֽׁי

Here the athnah is rather straightforward, dividing the verse into its two main parts: *David ran....* and *David went and said to Jonathan....*

In the first half of the first verset, *he ran* and *David* (וַיִּבְרַ֣ח דָּוִ֔ד) are taken as one whole—as if וַיִּבְרַ֣ח leans on or belongs to דָּוִ֔ד. In the second half, מִנָּיֹ֖ות is held back a bit by the ֖ from the בָּרָמָ֑ה. The passage could have read ֣ ֖ or even ֣ ֑ instead of ֖ ֑. By holding the two apart, the verse almost means *Naioth which is in Rama*; but the words *in Rama,* as pointed in the text, tell where Naioth is. The other pointing would have almost made it a single name, Naioth-of-Rama.

The second verset is cut into two divisions, the first ending with he word אָבִ֔יךָ. There was room for a certain amount of interpretation at this point. The sentence reads, roughly, "David came and said *X* because of *Y*." It would have been possible, therefore, to put the main stop after the word Jonathan. This would have balanced David's act of speaking against the words which he spoke. The text, however, chooses to find the center of gravity of David's words themselves and let the phrase *David said to Jonathan* be a minor appendage.

The introductory passage extends from the beginning of the second verset up to יְהֹונָתָ֗ן. The gershayim on וַיָּבֹ֣א holds itself back from the rest, while the two munaḥs in וַיֹּאמֶר | לִפְנֵי pull us on to their conclusion.

The vertical line in וַיֹּאמֶר | לִפְנֵי is to be taken together with the munaḥ accompanying the word preceding it. Together they are called a *legarmeh*. Legarmeh mitigates the leaning quality of the munaḥ to a certain extent; it indicates that ויאמר leans less strongly on לפני than לפני leans on יהונתן.

By the placement of zaqeph at אָבִ֫יךָ the two divisions of the second verset balance David's wonder against the grounds of that wonder. Notice that in the first division, the punctuator has treated the word מה with great care. In general, מה is a word in itself; but it may sometimes be treated as a proclytic—that is to say, it may be treated as part of the following word and hence receive no accent of its own. In our verse מה appears three times. The first appearance has its own accent to emphasize that it is a question. The punctuator was then able to treat each of the two remaining appearances as part of the word that follows, drumming in the question by setting a more rapid pace:

מֶה עָשִׂיתִי֙ מֶה־עֲוֹנִ֤י וּמֶה־חַטָּאתִי֙

Again, לפני is pulled toward, and leans on, אביך.

Note that in the second division, כִּי has been somewhat subordinated to מְבַקֵּק by writing ֤ ֥ ֖ rather than ֥ ֖ :

כִּ֤י מְבַקֵּ֖שׁ אֶת־נַפְשִׁ֑י

The latter pattern would have emphasized the *grounds* of David's doubt:

> And David … said … because *he seeks my life*?

But as that phrase is actually punctuated, it takes our mind away from David's reasoning process and turns us towards the things David is looking at:

> And David … said … *in that he seeks* my life?

As the reader can begin to see, the ta'amim, if they are taken to be grammatical in nature, tacitly contain a rather sophisticated understanding of grammatical analysis, although it is one quite different from our own. That difference in analysis reflects a difference in what each language considers to be a responsible statement. In English we would say: *David is King of Israel*, for in English, thoughts and words must be tied together by some form of the verb *to be*. In Hebrew, however, דוד מלך ישראל—*David King-of Israel*—is itself a responsible statement. Merely by placing words one after the other, the speaker or writer has made an assertion for which he can be held responsible. It therefore becomes critical to understand how these words interrelate—whether singly or in groups or in groups of groups of groups. It is as if we could write {David [(King of) Israel]}. It was also important to mark the kind of connection each word or group of words had with the next. Did they stand as equals as in *bread-and-butter*? Or did one lead up to the other, as in *House-of→ the King*?

It is interesting to note that taken in this way, *syntax*, the study of the way in which words come together to form statements, is merely the logical extension of *morphology*, the way in which roots or parts of roots came together to form words.

To give the reader a greater understanding and appreciation of the ta'amim, we have prepared Genesis 22:2 with interlinear translation so that the reader might grasp the whole in a single glance. Observe how the ֖ pulls the eye to the next word, how the ֒ often tends to pull us through the following word and on to the next. See how the "half-parentheses" hold ideas together and are often answered by things greater than themselves. Here, then, are the passages. Try reading them aloud, watching the shapes of the ta'amim as you go.

(even Isaac) (you love) (whom) (your single one) (your son) (Please take) (He said)

וַיֹּאמֶר קַח־נָא אֶת־בִּנְךָ אֶת־יְחִידְךָ אֲשֶׁר־אָהַבְתָּ אֶת־יִצְחָק

(as a sacrifice) (there) (and sacrifice him) (Moriah) (to the land of) (for yourself) (and go)

וְלֶךְ־לְךָ אֶל־אֶרֶץ הַמֹּרִיָּה וְהַעֲלֵהוּ שָׁם לְעֹלָה

.(to you) (I will say) (which) (the hills) (one of) (on)

עַל אַחַד הֶהָרִים אֲשֶׁר אֹמַר אֵלֶיךָ.

The trope is:

From the series ֬ ֜ ֨ , we can see that the geresh has been deleted and is only implied by the azla.

What can be said of the relationship between grammar and music, that two so radically different interpretations can be given to the same ta'amim? Consider the phrase above which might be rendered: (one⌐ of) (the⌐ mountains). Clearly the Hebrew leaning form demands completion, just as much as the dominant seventh chord. Perhaps one might not even be able to ask whether the people who established the ta'amim were hearing such expectation in the meaning of the words or in the cadence of their natural language. Perhaps the distinction itself did not really exist in the living speech. In the days when reading primarily meant reading aloud, did a question mark mean a question, or did it mean simply a slight rise in tone? Nevertheless, there is one great distinction between music and speech. A dominant seventh chord in G demands a C chord, but the phrase *a declaration of* does not demand the word *independence*. *War* would do as well, though words like *fish* or *triangle* would not. The phrase demands only a certain kind of word.

In our discussion of syntax, we suddenly seem to have fallen out of the realm of intentional grammar, back into the realm of formal grammar, and we run the risk of becoming like those children we imagined in Chapter 1—children who had become so fascinated by shapes and colors that they could no longer recognize the human in the picture. Undoubtedly, all these scraps of antique meanings, out of which language has been fashioned, are used and understood by the users to be pure forms; we cannot understand language without facing that. We can, however, avoid the blindness of formality by beginning the arduous task of seeing abstractions as abstractions through participating in the abstracting.

This rather long discussion came about because of the shift in vocalic mode in the last word of verse 20:5, which read ךְ instead of ךָ. The form is known as the pausal form. If the punctuator felt that a given pause was strong, he used the pausal form; otherwise, he used the regular form. This generally means that the pausal form is used for the silluq. The athnaḥ usually gets one, but not always. On the other hand, one can find occasions when even a r'bhia receives the pausal form. The pausal forms tend to be longer then the normal forms, though in some cases the change merely involves a shift in accent from the penultima the ultima. Quite often the pausal form is merely an older form that remained when the word was used in the pausal position. The following is a list of examples:

Normal	Pausal		Normal	Pausal
קָטַל	קָטָל		קֶשֶׁב	קָשֶׁב
אֱמֶת	אֱמֶת		דִּבֶּר	דִּבֵּר
יִקְטְלוּ	יִקְטֹלוּ		אֲנִי	אָנִי

14. I Samuel 20:5. Counting

וַיֹּ֣אמֶר דָּוִ֣ד אֶל־יְהוֹנָתָ֗ן הִנֵּֽה־חֹ֙דֶשׁ֙ מָחָ֔ר וְאָנֹכִ֛י 5
יָשֹׁב־אֵשֵׁ֥ב עִם־הַמֶּ֖לֶךְ לֶאֱכ֑וֹל וְשִׁלַּחְתַּ֙נִי֙ וְנִסְתַּרְתִּ֣י
בַשָּׂדֶ֔ה עַ֖ד הָעֶ֥רֶב הַשְּׁלִשִֽׁית

Notes on the reading:

חֹדֶשׁ

The root חדשׁ means *to be new or fresh* or, sometimes, it means *not yet*. Our word means *the new thing* par excellence, that is, *the new moon*. In later Hebrew it also comes to mean *month*.

מָחָר

מחר means *tomorrow*. No one, however, really believes that that is its root meaning; somehow the notion of *tomorrow* does not have enough of the smell of the earth to be a root concept. Some have suggested that it is a portmanteau word composed of יום (day) and the root אחר (*to come behind*). Others relate the word to an Assyrian root that means *to be in front of*.

יָשֹׁב־אֵשֵׁב

The root ישׁב is weak because the first letter is י. The main vocalic transformations are:

יִשֵׁב ← יֵשֵׁב
נִשֵׁב ← נוֹשֵׁב

In the first case, the חִרֶק (ִ)of the hollow state prefix, being followed by י, is taken to be an old חִרֶק and goes to צֵרֶה (ֵ). The second צֵרֶה came about through assonance, analogous to the forceful level. In the second case, recall that נִשֵׁב was originally נַישֵׁב and that יַ became וֹ when אַ went to וֹ.

ישׁב means *to dwell, to inhabit* or *to dwell together in a place* or even *to marry*. Most often it simply means *to sit*, but because of its ancestry it still retains a certain sense of community that is not found in the English word *sit*.

עִם

עִם comes from a root עמם that not used in Hebrew as a verb, but which still exists in Arabic; it means *to include*. It is closely related to the Hebrew word עַם, meaning *people*, in the sense of *nation* or *tribe*. That word goes back to an even earlier word meaning *kin*, and hence the whole of one's tribe, all that one trusts and loves. Our word עִם in Biblical Hebrew is the simple preposition *with*. To participate in the activity of Intentional Grammar means to see the abstract notion of *with* as arising out of family care and concern. Our objective is to develop the habit of reawakening the human thought that gave rise to these abstractions to which we find ourselves heir. We appropriate the notion of a preposition by thinking through the gap between its present formality and those antique feelings which were its progenitors.

הַמֶּלֶךְ

It is interesting to note that the word מלך or *king* goes back to an Akkadian word meaning *to advise*. That would imply that those who were first called מלך were called so on the basis of their ability to advise, rather than on account of strength, wealth, or stature.

לֶאֱכוֹל

The root אכל means *to eat*. It is weak because of the א, but if the reader bears in mind that א is not capable of existing in the shewa mode, the reader should have no problems with the vocalic changes involved. The principal ones are:

$$יְאֹכַל ← יָאֱכַל$$

and, in the first construction,

$$נְאֹכַל ← נָאֱכַל$$

In the normal form, לֶאֱכוֹל, we can see that we have the preposition *to* plus the hollow state of the verb. Together they form the infinitive. There is surely no necessity for the infinitive to begin with the preposition *to*, and indeed many languages do not work that way. However the fact that two such diverse languages as Hebrew and English share this characteristic would seem to call for some rational account. Our desire for such an account reveals that we regard languages as existing somewhere between the universally necessary and the merely arbitrary. A language cannot be wholly arbitrary or we could not use it to communicate; it cannot be universal or we would all speak the same language.

The presence of *to* in the infinitive can best be understood by considering the words with which we tend to use the infinitive: *I want to..., I like to..., I didn't think to....* Each of these phrases seems in one way or another to take the infinitive as some kind of goal: a wanting is a wanting directed *to* or *towards* something, a liking is a liking directed *to* or *towards* something. But what of the phrase *seems to,* itself? There are many such phrases in which the *to* of the infinitive does not imply a *towards* in the sense of a goal, but rather a *putting to* for purposes of comparison.

In some such way it seems that the infinitive, more clearly than the future tense, captures the spirit of the hollow state as being a *to* or a *not yet.*

וְשִׁלַּחְתַּנִי

The dagesh in the ל indicates that we are at the forceful level. The full paradigm is:

Ground Forceful Level, Active (פִּעֵל)

Hollow		Solid		
יְקַטְּלוּ	יְקַטֵּל	קִטְּלוּ	קִטֵּל	3rd masc.
תְּקַטֵּלְנָה	תְּקַטֵּל	קִטְּלוּ	קִטְּלָה	3rd fem.
תְּקַטְּלוּ	תְּקַטֵּל	קִטַּלְתֶּם	קִטַּלְתָּ	2nd masc.
תְּקַטֵּלְנָה	תְּקַטְּלִי	קִטַּלְתֶּן	קִטַּלְתְּ	2nd fem.
נְקַטֵּל	אֲקַטֵּל	קִטַּלְנוּ	קִטַּלְתִּי	1st c.

Ground Forceful Level, Passive (פֻּעַל)

Hollow		Solid		
יְקַטְּלוּ	יְקֻטַּל	קֻטְּלוּ	קֻטַּל	3rd masc.
תְּקֻטַּלְנָה	תְּקֻטַּל	קֻטְּלוּ	קֻטְּלָה	3rd fem.
תְּקֻטְּלוּ	תְּקֻטַּל	קֻטַּלְתֶּם	קֻטַּלְתָּ	2nd masc.
תְּקֻטַּלְנָה	תְּקֻטְּלִי	קֻטַּלְתֶּן	קֻטַּלְתְּ	2nd fem.
נְקֻטַּל	אֲקֻטַּל	קֻטַּלְנוּ	קֻטַּלְתִּי	1st c.

The root שׁלח is irregular because of the guttural in the third position. The main vocalic changes stem from the fact that the gutturals prefer to follow a פָּתָח (ַ) rather than a צֵרֶה (ֵ). The main examples are:

$$\text{יְשָׁלֵח} \leftarrow \text{יְשָׁלַח}$$
$$\text{שָׁלֵח} \leftarrow \text{שָׁלַח}$$

Originally the root may have meant *to set free*, a meaning it still has in a few Biblical passages; but in general it has the more intense and direct sense *to send*.

וְנִסְתַּרְתִּי

The Semitic root סתר means *to hide* or *to conceal*, but the ground form does not exist in Hebrew although it still does in several other Semitic languages. The נ is a signal that our word is in the first construction; and since it has retained the original sense of the first construction, the whole word וְנִסְתַּרְתִּי means *and I will hide myself*.

בַּשָּׂדֶה

שָׂדֶה means *field* or *countryside*, but not much more seems to be known about the word, though it might go back to a root שׂדד, *to harrow*.

עַד

עַד is a preposition related to a cluster of roots:

count, add	עדד
pass on, advance	עדה
go about, return	עוד

From עדה, *it advances to*, arises the sense *it is to*, and thence our present word עַד, meaning *until*.

הָעֶרֶב

The word עֶרֶב means *evening*. However, its origins are somewhat obscure due to an embarrassment of riches. Part of the problem is that the earlier Semitic tongues had more phonemes than does Hebrew; and indeed, the modern Arabic alphabet still contains many of them. As a consequence, two quite distinct roots may have been conflated into one when they came into the Hebrew language. In this and other cases, several early Semitic roots seem reasonable candidates for the origin of עֶרֶב; and given the strange turns that human thought can take, there is no guarantee that the most reasonable origin is the actual origin.

The most likely source is an Akkadian root meaning *to go down*. That would imply that evening is the time of the going down of the sun. But there is also an Egyptian root, one that commonly occurs in Hebrew also, and which means *mixture*. Evening could have been seen as the time of the mixture of day and night, or as we say, *twilight*.

הַשְּׁלִשִׁית

הַשְּׁלִשִׁית means *the third*. There is more to be said about this particular word, but first we must learn to count.

Numbers

	Masculine		Feminine	
	Absolute	*Leaning*	*Absolute*	*Leaning*
1	אֶחָד	אַחַד	אַחַת	אַחַת
2	שְׁנַיִם	שְׁנֵי	שְׁתַּיִם	שְׁתֵּי
3	שְׁלשָׁה	שְׁלשֶׁת	שָׁלשׁ	שְׁלשׁ
4	אַרְבָּעָה	אַרְבַּעַת	אַרְבַּע	אַרְבַּע
5	חֲמִשָּׁה	חֲמֵשֶׁת	חָמֵשׁ	חֲמֵשׁ
6	שִׁשָּׁה	שֵׁשֶׁת	שֵׁשׁ	שֵׁשׁ
7	שִׁבְעָה	שִׁבְעַת	שֶׁבַע	שְׁבַע
8	שְׁמנָה	שְׁמנַת	שְׁמנֶה	שְׁמנֶה
9	תִּשְׁעָה	תִּשְׁעַת	תֵּשַׁע	תְּשַׁע
10	עֲשָׂרָה	עֲשֶׂרֶת	עֶשֶׂר	עֶשֶׂר
11	אַחַד עָשָׂר		אַחַת עֶשְׂרֵה	
12	שְׁנֵים עָשָׂר		שְׁתֵּים עֶשְׂרֵה	
13	שְׁלשָׁה עָשָׂר		שְׁלשׁ עֶשְׂרֵה	
⋮	⋮		⋮	
20	עֶשְׂרִים			
21	עֶשְׂרִים וְאֶחָד			
30	שְׁלשִׁים			

Numbers

Masculine and Feminine

	Absolute	Leaning
100	מֵאָה	מְאַת
200	מָאתַיִם	–
300	שְׁלֹשׁ מֵאוֹת	–
1000	אֶלֶף	–
2000	אַלְפַּיִם	–
3000	שְׁלֹשֶׁת אֲלָפִים	–
10,000	רְבָבָה	–
20,000	שְׁתֵּי רִבּוֹת	–

The most striking feature of the number system is that the masculine numbers from three to ten are feminine in form and the feminine numbers masculine in form, which suggests that the numbers were originally feminine nouns. Shreds of such a way of thought still exist in our own language in such expressions as *the six of them.* That would imply that ideas more analogous to words like *trio, quartet,* and *quintet* were prior to the words *three, four,* and *five.* In that earlier stage, the leaning form would normally have been used; one would not say *three men,* but *a trio of men.*

By now we all have learned from the anthropologists that there are languages that distinguish only *one* and *many.* Other languages go as far as *one, two, many* (reflecting the fact that a *pair* is a striking thing, a new thing that will not let one forget the old). Still other languages can articulate a *triad,* perhaps originally by seeing *father, mother* and *child* as a family. Once the "child" has been seen as holding the "family" together, there is even room in thought for a stranger—a fourth.

It seems, however, that once a language goes beyond five or six, thought ceases to grasp collections as wholes but must develop the idea of succession. If someone finds a way of thinking much beyond *five,* he must have come to a different feeling for number, one that at least hints at the notion of a system based on succession. An adequate understanding of the

Hebrew numbering system, however, requires some feeling for those older ways of counting.

Evidently, someone who counts *one, two, three* and then stops because the rest is *more*, is not doing the same that you or I do when we count to three. Nevertheless, some of the old ways are still alive in our thought. Musicians rarely count beyond four.[1] In this, they may be exhibiting a much deeper inner sense of the individual character of each number than do most mathematicians.

Today we speak with ease of a pair, a trio, or a quartet, but a nonet tends to boggle the mind, while the word centet sounds downright ridiculous. While it is true that the number ninety-nine is the predecessor of one hundred, and hence is not equal to the number one hundred, yet no one can hold in mind the difference between a ninety-nine and a hundred the way we grasp the difference between a one and a two, or even that between a two and a three.

As you can see, Hebrew's way of numbering or counting things comprises a conglomerate of discrete insights and even conflicting ways of reaching out to find verbal expression for thought. In this it resembles other languages; think of the sudden appearance of *quatre-vingt* in French, or our own *eleven*. Perhaps the most remarkable facet to this affair is that in the face of so many radical changes in the ways people have thought about number, there is distinct agreement among the Semitic languages in the final form which the numbers took. That would imply that those changes had already happened before Proto-Semitic broke up into its various branches.[2] This remarkable level of agreement among the Semitic languages can be seen in the following chart:

---

1. When a musical measure contains more than three or four beats, performers tend to break it up into twos and threes.

2. Remember that in Arabic, ת and ת are distinct letters. Note also that the Arabic letter ה, used only for feminine endings, is pronounced as if it were ת. This seems to imply that sometime before they learned to write, at least some speakers of Arabic also dropped the final feminine ת; they would have found it natural to write ה as in Hebrew. Then there must have been a reform, either on the part of those who still pronounced the ת, or on the part of some who felt a need to return to what seemed to them to be a truer form of the language. I suspect that their desire to return was tempered by the established custom, and so they invented the letter ה.

Semitic Cardinal Numbers

	Akkadian	Ugaritic	Hebrew	Syriac	Arabic	Amharic
1 masc.	עֶשְׁתֵּן	אחד	אֶחָד	חַד	וָאחִדֹ	אָחָדُو
fem.	עֶשְׁתֶּת	אחת	אֶחָת	חֲדָא	וָאחִדָה	אָחַתִּי
2 masc.	שֵׁן	תמם	שְׁנַיִם	תְּרֵי	אתְנָאנ	כְּלָא
fem.	שִׁתָּ		שְׁתַּיִם	תַּרְתֵּי	אתְנָתָאנ	כְּלַאתִי
3 masc.	שָׁלָאשֶׁת	תלת	שְׁלֹשָׁה	תְּלָתָא	תַּלָאתָה	שָׁלַשְׁתֵּוֹ
fem.	שָׁלָשׁ		שְׁלֹשׁ	תְּלָת	תַּלָאת	שָׁלָשׁ
4 masc.	אֶרְבֶּת	ארבע	אַרְבָּעָה	אַרְבְּעָא	אַרְבָּעָה	אַרְבַּעְתֵּוֹ
fem.	אַרְבַּע		אַרְבַּע	אַרְבַּע	אַרְבַּע	אַרְבַּע
5 masc.	חַמְשֶׁת	חמש	חֲמִשָּׁה	חַמְשָׁא	חַמְסָה	חַמִּשְׁתֵּוֹ
fem.	חָמֶשׁ		חָמֵשׁ	חַמֵשׁ	חַמְס	חַמֵּשׁ
6 masc.	שֵׁשֶׁת	תת	שִׁשָּׁה	שֵׁתָּ	סִתָּה	שֶׁדֶשְׁתֵּוֹ
fem.	[שֵׁשׁ]		שֵׁשׁ	שֵׁת	סִתּ	שִׁשּׁו
7 masc.	שֶׁבֶּת	שבע	שִׁבְעָה	שַׁבְעָא	סַבְעָה	שַׁבְעַתֵּוֹ
fem.	שֶׁב		שֶׁבַע	שְׁבַע	סַבְע	שַׁבְעו
8 masc.	שָׁמָאנִית	תמן	שְׁמֹנָה	תְּמָנְיָא	תַּמָאנִיָה	שָׁמָאנִיתֵּוֹ
fem.	שָׁמֶן		שְׁמֹנֶה	תְּמָנֵ	תַּמָאן	שָׁמָאנִי
9 masc.	תֵּשִׁית	תשע	תִּשְׁעָה	תֵּשְׁעָא	תִּסְעָה	תֵּשְׁעַתֵּוֹ
fem.	תֵּשׁ		תֵּשַׁע	תְּשַׁע	תִּסְע	תֵּשְׁעו
10 masc.	עֶשְׂרֶת	עשר	עֲשָׂרָה	עֶשְׂרָא	עַשְׂרָה	עָשָׂרְתֵּוֹ
fem.	עֶשֶׂר		עֶשֶׂר	עֶשַׂר	עַשְׂר	עָשְׂרו
20 c.	עֶשְׂרָא	עשרמ	עֶשְׂרִים	עֶשְׂרִין	עַשְׂרֹנַ	עָשְׂרָא
30 c.	שָׁלָאשָׁא	תלתמ	שְׁלֹשִׁים	תְּלָתִין	תַּלָאתוּן	שָׁלָאשָׁא

In each of these languages, the grammatical form of the words for *one* and *two* agrees in gender with the objects to which they are applied. *One* and *two* seem in this way to be nearer to things than are *three* and *four*. Let us consider these numbers, and some others, in turn.

One. The root אחד has a close relative, יחד, which means *to be together, to be united.* In English it seems clear that such a word as *unite* is derivative from our notion of unit, or *uno*, or one. In Hebrew, however, it is not so clear which is the more fundamental thought: whether things are one because they have come together, or whether being together is being like a one. To answer the question whether יחד came from אחד or the reverse may prove to be neither possible nor important. But even to have asked the question is to begin to understand why "one" might not have the same kind of being as "a triad of...."

Two. The word שְׁנַיִם is dual in form, and hence describes the object to which it is attached. For that reason it agrees with the object in gender and does not have the independence we find in the higher numbers. The root is שנת, and the feminine form, שְׁתַּיִם (which, contrary to all rules, has a dagesh after a moving shewa) shows how deeply the missing נ was felt. The root itself can mean *to change*. It is of course, tempting to assume that the notion of *change* lies somewhere behind the earliest speakers' insight into duality, but that must remain conjectural.

Three. The root שלש is also the root from which derives the word for *chain*. Three is beyond two because there is something in the middle that ties them together.

Four. The root רבע means *to stretch out*, and given the expression *the four corners of the earth*, it is not impossible that there is some etymological connection between the two.

We should of course like to go further, but the origins of the Semitic number-words from five through nine (if indeed they had distinct origins) have all been lost. The same obscurity characterizes the corresponding number-words in Chinese. Such observations would seem to strengthen the notion that the numbers beyond four are part of a newer concept of number.

Ten. In Arabic there is a root עשר which means *to assemble, to gather*, or *to unite*. This would suggest that *ten* was seen as the first assemblage, or as the new unit. The word probably goes back to a time when shepherds counted their sheep by making a scratch each time a sheep went by. The scratches could be gathered into units of tens in a way that could not be done with the sheep themselves. Some innovative mind must have been the first to have grasped that, yet we rarely stop to take note of this kind of insight.

Twenty. עֶשְׂרִים has the form of the plural of ten. It thus expresses "tens" (the "two" being understood); or perhaps it was once the "double-ten."

Thirty. The use of the plural שְׁלֹשִׁים for thirty cannot be the same kind of thing. The word could not have meant "two three's," although it has that form; and it is not likely to have meant "ten three's" to its originators. In Akkadian and Ugaritic we have already seen plurality expressed by bigness (page 62). Here, I suggest, the inverse has occurred, so that שְׁלֹשִׁים means "a big three," that is, a three made of the big units.

The word in our verse is שְׁלִשִׁית, the feminine form of the ordinal number *third* (the masculine is שְׁלִשִׁי). In contrast to the cardinal numbers, the ordinal numbers always agree in form with the gender of the object and do not have the independence of the cardinals. Note that because of the final long *I*-mode ending יִ-, the old feminine ending ת did not soften to a final הָ-.

Semitic Ordinal Numbers

	Akkadian	Ugaritic	Hebrew	Syriac	Arabic	Amharic
First	מַחְרֵו		רִאשׁוֹן	קַדְמָאיָא	אֹול	קָדָאמִי
Second	שָׁנֵו	תן	שֵׁנִי	תֶּנְיָאנָא	תָאנִי	כָּלֵא
Third	שַׁלֵשׁ	תלת	שְׁלִישִׁי	תְּלִיתָאיָא	תָאלֵת	שָׁאלֵשׁ

As is the case in most languages, the first ordinal number is totally unrelated to the first cardinal. In English even the word *second* is unrelated to the word *two,* as well. *First* is related to Sanskrit *paros, to be in front of,* and *second* to a Sanskrit word meaning *to follow.*

The Akkadian root מחר also means *to be in front of,* as do the words in Arabic and Syriac/Amharic. The Hebrew root ראשׁ means *head.*

15. I Samuel 20:6

‏6 אִם־פָּקֹד יִפְקְדֵ֫נִי אָבִ֑יךָ וְאָמַרְתָּ נִשְׁאֹל נִשְׁאַל מִמֶּ֫נִּי
דָוִד לָרוּץ בֵּית־לֶ֫חֶם עִירֹו כִּי זֶ֫בַח הַיָּמִים שָׁם
לְכָל־הַמִּשְׁפָּחָה׃‏

Notes on the reading:

‏אִם‏

‏אִם‏, cognate to ‏הֵן‏, is etymologically part of a whole cluster[1] of words centering around the third-person pronoun, the demonstrative pronoun, and the word for *here*. From beginning as a word that points out or calls our attention to something, it must have taken on the less spatially oriented meaning of *suppose*. By the time of Biblical Hebrew it had come to signify *if*.

‏פָּקֹד יִפְקְדֵ֫נִי אָבִ֑יךָ‏

In the ground form ‏פקד‏ means *to pay attention to, to observe, to check up on*.

‏וְאָמַרְתָּ נִשְׁאֹל נִשְׁאַל מִמֶּ֫נִּי דָוִד‏

The ground form of ‏שאל‏ means *to demand, to inquire*, or *to ask*. The first construction was still in the old style, and so it had the general sense of *asking for oneself*; but by Biblical times the first construction of the word had narrowed down to the specific meaning *to ask for leave of absence*.

‏לָרוּץ בֵּית־לֶ֫חֶם‏

The root ‏רוץ‏ once meant *to run to the aid of...*; but by Biblical times it usually meant simply *to run*, and one can even find the expression ‏לרוץ מין‏—*to run from*. However, ‏רוץ‏ can still bear the meaning *to run to...*, as is the case in our passage.

The root ‏רוץ‏ is weak because of the ‏ו‏ in the middle position. In

---

1. Recall the discussion of clusters on pages 39–42 in Chapter 5.

general, the major changes arise from the fact that the ו tends to turn vocalic:

קוֹל ← קָל

קוֹלָה ← קָלָה

יָקוֹל ← יָקוֹל

נִקוֹל ← נָקוֹל

הֵקִיל ← הֻקְוִיל

קוֹלֵל ← קֻל²

You can see the results for yourself. The ו became vocalic and coalesced with the A-sound. Usually the A-mode does win out, as happened in the formation of רַצְתִּי from רוץ; but sometimes the ו predominates, as was the case in forming בּוֹשְׁתִּי from בוש. When the ו was dropped from the hollow state the number of syllables decreased, and the law of lightening no longer applied. Hence one finds נָקוֹל instead of נְקוֹל.

The rather strange form of the forceful level, קוֹלֵל, can only be understood if one supposes that when the ו became vocalic, the speakers missed the feeling of the double letter. The specific form was then attracted to the form which arises when the second and third root letters are in fact the same.

For a clear comparison, we include the same forms for a root קלל. These roots are often called double-ע roots:

קָלַל ← קָל

קָלְלָה ← קַלָּה

יָקֹל ← יִקְלֹל

נָקַל ← נִקְלַל

הֵקֵל ← הַקְלִיל

לָרוּץ בֵּית־לֶחֶם

Note that בית לחם, *Bethlehem*, is treated as the direct object of לרוץ without any intervening preposition.

עִירוֹ

עיר comes from an Akkadian root which originally meant *hill* but later came to mean *city*. Its history thus would seem to parallel

---

2. Here ו is not a shuruq but a waw dagesh, indicating that קֻל has the forceful level.

the change in German from *berg* to *burg*; the idea behind the change seems pretty clear in both cases.

כִּי זֶבַח הַיָּמִים

So far as one can tell, the root זבח, even when traced back to Akkadian, always had the double meaning of *to slaughter* and *to sacrifice*, and it appears impossible to discover whether the secular or the religious intent was prior.

The word יום underwent the following transformation:

$$יוֹם → יוֹם$$
$$יָמִים → יוֹמִים$$

Like its English counterpart, יום can refer to the time of daylight, or to one complete cycle of the sun. "Therefore shall you remain at the door of the Tent of Meeting day and night seven *days*…" (Leviticus 8:35).

שָׁם

The word means *there*, but the present writer has no satisfactory account of it.

לְכָל

The root כלל means *to be complete*, as in the verse, "Thus the heavens and the earth were *finished*, and all the host of them" (Genesis 2:1). As one might have anticipated from our discussion of רוץ, the root כלל is closely related to another root, כול, which means *to comprehend* or *to contain*. Our word, כָּל, is the leaning form of the word כּוֹל. Strictly, it signifies *the collected whole of…*, though it is usually best translated simply as *all* or *every*. Since our word is a leaning form, the reader should be able to tell that the vocalic mode is a short *O* rather than a long *A*.

הַמִּשְׁפָּחָה

משפחה is a noun meaning *family*. The root שפח, *to pour*, belongs to a cluster of roots including שפע, *to flow abundantly*; and the vocalic pattern is מַקְטָלָה.

As in participles, so here too the prefix מ is a shred of the word מָה, *what*. Unlike participles, however, nouns formed in this way tend to take on special meanings of their own that cannot readily be derived from the meaning of the verbal root.

Other examples illustrating this vocalic pattern are shown in the following chart.

ROOT		NOUN	
בצר	to cut off / fortify	מִבְצָר	a fortified city
גדל	to be big / to become big	מִגְדָּל	a tower
גרש	to cast out	מִגְרָשׁ	a plot of land outside the city
דרש	to search out	מִדְרָשׁ	an exposition
כבר	to twist	מִכְבָּר	lattice-work
מכר	to sell	מִמְכָּר	a sale / merchandise
משל	to rule	מֶמְשָׁל	dominion
משק	[meaning unknown]	מֶמְשָׁק	a possession
סחר	to travel	מִסְחָר	trade
ספר	to count	מִסְפָּר	a number of...
פלט	to escape	מִפְלָט	an escape
פקד	to visit / to muster / to check up on	מִפְקָד	an appointment / a census
צוה	to command	מִצְוָה	a commandment
ספח	to join	מִסְפָּחָה	a quilt
לחם	to eat / to fight	מִלְחָמָה	a war
שפח	to pour out	מִשְׁפָּחָה	a family

16. I Samuel 20:7

7 אִם־כֹּה יֹאמַר טוֹב שָׁלוֹם לְעַבְדֶּךָ וְאִם־חָרֹה יֶחֱרֶה לוֹ דַּע כִּי־כָלְתָה הָרָעָה מֵעִמּוֹ

Notes on the reading:

כֹּה

The כ has a rather complicated history. It begins with the root כון which means *to stand* or *to be firm or stable*. In a slightly altered form it might mean *to establish* and hence it develops also the meaning *to exist*. The word כֵּן, going back to an original כִּין, means *thus* or *so* in the sense of *in accordance with a clear and definite way*, as in the verse, "And it was so" (Genesis 1:7). In this verse we must understand the word *so* to have the same significance that it does in the phrase, "He likes everything to be just so."

Another member of this cluster of roots is כֹּה, meaning *this way, thus,* or *now*. Sometimes it degenerates into the prefix כְּ, meaning *thus,* or *about* in the sense of "approximately," as in the phrase *about ten days*. כְּ sometimes means *like,* as in *like a lion*; hence, if used with a verb, it can mean *as if*. Sometimes it can mean *according to,* as in the phrase *according to the words of…*. All these meanings share the implication of a standard of straightness and steadfastness according to which things may be measured, and this steadfastness seems closely related to the certainty of presentness.

Some writers have argued that this sense of being steadfast and present may lie behind the כ in the first person pronoun אנכי (*I*), but that seems quite doubtful to me.

טוֹב

טוֹב means *good* or *pleasant* or *joyful*. Its usage is as wide as the human mind and imagination allows. Its plural is טוֹבִים, which would imply that its root is טאב, the א having become vocalic according to the process described in Chapter 5.

שָׁלוֹם

The root שלם means *to be intact, to be whole,* or *to be in good health.* In the forceful level it has a causative sense to it and means *to make whole* or *to make good.* From there it comes to mean *to pay a debt* or simply *to pay* (for anything). Buying and selling, then, was first considered less a matter of mercantilism than of giving and restoring.

Our word, שָׁלוֹם means *welfare* or *well-being,* and in the case of a whole people it is equivalent to our word *peace.* It should also be noted that our own word *pay* goes back to the Latin *pacare,* to pacify or appease, and hence it too is related to the Latin word for peace, which is *pax.*

לְעָבְדֶּךָ

The root עבד bears the meanings *to work, to slave,* or *to serve,* including *to serve God*—both in the sense of daily action and in the sense of ritual. The word עֶבֶד means *servant,* and it can partake of any of the senses of עבד.

יֶחֱרֶה

The root חרה means *to burn.* It is doubly irregular. On the one hand, since the ח cannot be pronounced in the shewa mode, the hireq is shared between the י and the ח so that יְחָ becomes יֶחֱ. On the other hand, as we saw in the case of גלה, the true root is חרי. The י is then taken to be vocalic, so that one has the form חָרִיתִי; at the end of a word, however, it is shortened so that we have יֶחֱרֶה.

Quite often the subject of the verb is *his nose,* אַפּוֹ; and even when not present it is always implied. The Biblical expression *he burnt,* or *his nose burnt* means *he was fuming,* or *he was angry.* For an example, see Numbers 11:1.

דַּע

דַּע is the imperative form of ידע, a root we have seen before and unfortunately a quite irregular one. The regular form is קְטֹל. Now in general, modality is conveyed in Hebrew by varying the time it takes to speak the word; in this case, the imperative form תִּקְטֹל has been shortened to קְטֹל that it might be snapped out the more quickly. The other forms of imperatives are:

Imperative

3rd construction	2nd construction	1st construction	Ground	
הַקְטֵל		הַקְטֵל	קְטֹל	sing. masc.
הַקְטִילִי		הַקְטֵל	קִטְלִי	sing. fem.
הַקְטִלוּ		הַקְטִילוּ	קִטְלוּ	plur. masc.
הַקְטֵלְנָה		הַקְטֵלְנָה	קְטֹלְנָה	plur. fem.

	forceful		forceful	
	הִתְקַטֵּל		קַטֵּל	sing. masc.
	הִתְקַטְּלִי		קַטְּלִי	sing. fem.
	הִתְקַטְּלוּ		קַטְּלוּ	plur. masc.
	הִתְקַטֵּלְנָה		קַטֵּלְנָה	plur. fem.

Note that in the case of our word יָדַע, the י has also been dropped in order to shorten the word even more. Similarly, the imperative of the word הלך is simply לֵך, *go*! Although in these examples one notices that both י and ה are weak, this does not imply a general rule of dropping a weak letter; quite the contrary, a root letter is almost always retained intact. דַּע and לֵך are special cases, perhaps because they are words commonly commanded.

The sharpness of the imperative is sometimes mitigated by the addition of an extra syllable, producing the more polite form קָטוֹלָה. Under even more polite circumstances one may add the particle נָא, which transforms a demand into a request. No one is quite sure what the root of נָא is, but it occurs to me that it might come from the root נאה, meaning *beautiful*—the way German appends the word *schön* (beautiful) to produce *dankeschön*—an emphatic form of "thank you."

Correspondingly, there is a lengthened and somewhat more polite form for the first person: אֶקְטֹל becomes אֶקְטְלָה. In many ways this marks a return to what we have taken to be the original sense of the hollow state, as having more to do with the possible and the desirable than with the future as such. It is comparable to our construction *O that I might...*, or *May I...*, either in the sense of asking permission or of offering to do something for someone else. Lengthening may also express a desired outcome, as it does in the verse, "Bring me venison … that I might eat (וְאֹכֵלָה)"

(Genesis 27:7) The polite first person form may also be accompanied by the word נָא.

There is also a shortened form of the third person, though the third person imperfect is already so short the change is more by implication than by anything explicit in the text. Still, advantage can sometimes be taken of a weak letter. The word יִגְלֶה (verse 20:2) would shorten to יִגֶל. Its imperative-like force is often captured in English by the word *let*, as in *let there be light*. This form too may be followed or preceded by נָא.

כֶלְתָה

This is a feminine verbal form from the root כול.

הָרָעָה

It is difficult to find an English equivalent to the word רעה (fem. sing.) since it does not quite mean either *bad* or *evil*. A chair that wants a leg is a bad chair, but it is not, for all that, evil. The distinction we make in English between bad and evil presupposes a radical distinction between faults in human beings and faults in the world about them. Although the word רע (masc. sing.) similarly presupposes the existence of man, things are רע not because they are done by man, but because men suffer on account of them. Wild beasts are not evil, but they are רעה when they threaten human existence, as in this verse:

> Come now therefore, and let us slay him, and throw him into some pit, and we will say, Some wicked (רעה) beast has devoured him; and we shall see what will become of his dreams. (Genesis 37:20)

Inanimate things can be רעה:

> And it came to pass, as they were eating of the pottage, that they cried out, and said, O you man of God, there is death in the pot. And they could not eat of it. But he said, Then bring meal. And he cast it into the pot; and he said, Pour out for the people, that they may eat. And there was nothing harmful (רעה) in the pot. (II Kings 4:40–41)

מֵעִמּוֹ

Think of מִן + עִמּוֹ.

17. I Samuel 20:8–9

8 וְעָשִׂ֤יתָ חֶ֨סֶד֙ עַל־עַבְדֶּ֔ךָ כִּ֚י בִּבְרִ֣ית יְהֹוָ֔ה הֵבֵ֥אתָ
אֶֽת־עַבְדְּךָ֖ עִמָּ֑ךְ וְאִם־יֶשׁ־בִּ֤י עָוֺן֙ הֲמִיתֵ֣נִי אַ֔תָּה
וְעַד־אָבִ֥יךָ לָמָּה־זֶּ֖ה תְבִיאֵֽנִי׃

Notes on the reading:

חֶסֶד

The word חֶסֶד means *kindness* or *goodness*.

בִּבְרִית

The root ברי in Akkadian means *to bind*, but our word is the only word in Hebrew from that root. It is a feminine noun, originally of the form בְּרִיתְ; but note that since י has become vocalic, the ת has not gone to ה. The word itself means *covenant* as it does in Akkadian, where it can also mean *fetter*.

הֵבֵאתָ

הֵבֵאתָ is the third construction on the root בוא which, as we saw in verse 20:1, means *to come*. In the third construction, then, it means *to cause to come*, or more simply, *to bring*.

The regular paradigm of the third constriction is:

Third Construction Active (הִפְעִיל)

Hollow		Solid		
Plur.	Sing.	Plur.	Sing.	
יַקְטִילוּ	יַקְטִיל	הַקְטִילוּ	הַקְטִיל	3rd masc.
תַּקְטֵלְנָה	תַּקְטִיל	הַקְטִילוּ	הַקְטִילָה	3rd fem.
תַּקְטִילוּ	תַּקְטִיל	הִקְטַלְתֶּם	הִקְטַלְתָּ	2nd masc.
תַּקְטֵלְנָה	תַּקְטִילִי	הִקְטַלְתֶּן	הִקְטַלְתְּ	2nd fem.
נַקְטִיל	אַקְטִיל	הִקְטַלְנוּ	הִקְטַלְתִּי	1st c.

Third Construction Passive (הָפְעַל)

Hollow		*Solid*		
Plur.	Sing.	Plur.	Sing.	
יֻקְטְלוּ	יָקְטַל	הָקְטְלוּ	הָקְטַל	3rd masc.
תֻּקְטַלְנָה	תֻּקְטַל	הָקְטְלוּ	הָקְטְלָה	3rd fem.
תֻּקְטְלוּ	תֻּקְטַל	הָקְטַלְתֶּם	הָקְטַלְתָּ	2nd masc.
תֻּקְטַלְנָה	תֻּקְטְלִי	הָקְטַלְתֶּן	הָקְטַלְתְּ	2nd fem.
נֻקְטַל	אֻקְטַל	הָקְטַלְנוּ	הָקְטַלְתִּי	1st c.

From what has been said about the passive, one might have expected הֻקְטַל. Instead, at a rather early stage the short *U* (הֻ) went to a short *O* (הָ). Nevertheless, one finds instances of הֻקְטַל fairly often.

Our word הֻבֵאתָ is doubly weak. The regular form would have been הֻבְוַאתָ, but the ב inherits the vocalic complex, forcing the short ḥireq to a long ṣere, absorbing the ו.

יֵשׁ

The word יֵשׁ, here shortened to יֶשׁ because of its closeness to the word that follows it, goes back to an Akkadian root ישׁו, which meant *to have* or *to possess*. In Hebrew it exists in this form only and has the sense of the German expression *es gibt*, or the English expression *there is*.

הֲמִיתֵנִי

הֲמִיתֵנִי is the third construction on the ground form מות.

9 וַיֹּאמֶר יְהוֹנָתָן חָלִילָה לָּךְ כִּי | אִם־יָדֹעַ אֵדַע כִּי־כָלְתָה הָרָעָה מֵעִם אָבִי לָבוֹא עָלֶיךָ וְלֹא אֹתָהּ אַגִּיד לָךְ:

Notes on the reading:

אַגִּיד

The dagesh in the ג should indicate to the reader that the root is נגד, the א that the speaker is the doer, and the י that we are in the third, or causative, construction. The earliest meaning of the root seems to have been related to *a high place*, but it soon came to mean *to be conspicuous*, and hence to be *before* or even *against* in the sense of *being opposed to*. In the third construction it means *to put something before someone* or. more simply, *to tell*.

18. I Samuel 20:10–12

10 וַיֹּ֤אמֶר דָּוִד֙ אֶל־יְה֣וֹנָתָ֔ן מִ֣י יַגִּ֣יד לִ֔י א֖וֹ מַה־יַּעַנְךָ֥ אָבִ֖יךָ קָשָֽׁה׃

11 וַיֹּ֤אמֶר יְהֽוֹנָתָן֙ אֶל־דָּוִ֔ד לְכָ֖ה וְנֵצֵ֣א הַשָּׂדֶ֑ה וַיֵּצְא֥וּ שְׁנֵיהֶ֖ם הַשָּׂדֶֽה׃

12 וַיֹּ֨אמֶר יְהוֹנָתָ֜ן אֶל־דָּוִ֗ד יְהֹוָ֞ה אֱלֹהֵ֤י יִשְׂרָאֵל֙ כִּֽי־אֶחְקֹ֣ר אֶת־אָבִ֗י כָּעֵ֤ת ׀ מָחָר֙ הַשְּׁלִשִׁ֔ית וְהִנֵּה־ט֖וֹב אֶל־דָּוִ֑ד וְלֹֽא־אָ֗ז אֶשְׁלַ֤ח אֵלֶ֙יךָ֙ וְגָלִ֖יתִי אֶת־אָזְנֶֽךָ׃

Notes on the reading:

יַּעַנְךָ

The Akkadian root ענו originally meant *to change* or *to turn around*. By the time of Biblical Hebrew, the root seems to have split and to have developed in two different directions. From the notion of *turning* came the notion of *returning*, and hence the word can mean *to answer*. On the other hand, the notion *turning* also led to the thought of *turning on* and hence to *afflicting*, or *doing violence to*. There are many passages, including the present one, in which each meaning can subtly be heard within the other. For example, Ecclesiastes 1:13 may be read as:

> And I gave my heart to seek and search out by wisdom concerning all things that are done under heaven; it is a hard task that God has given to the sons of man *to answer* concerning it.

Or as:

> And I gave my heart to seek and search out by wisdom concerning all things that are done under heaven; it is a hard task that God has given to the sons of man *to torture* him with it.

קָשָׁה

Hard, severe, or fierce.

לְכָה

At the end of Chapter 16 we noted a rather polite form in which verbs sometimes appear. לְכָה is that polite form of לֵךְ, the second person singular imperative of the root הלך. The ground form means *to go on foot*. Note that the ה, rather than taking a ḥatuph, was simply dropped.

אֶחְקֹר

חקר means *to investigate*. Such investigation may or may not require eyes, but it always requires thought.

עֵת

The word עֵת means *a time* in the sense of a special occasion like *a good time*, or *a time to sow and a time to reap*; but never does it mean *time on your hands*. It cannot be long and it cannot be short, and it certainly is not something to be measured by a clock. Although in Hebrew one may ask, *How many days?*, there is almost no way to ask, *How much time?* However it is very exciting to find in the Book of Daniel—the last book of the Bible to be written—the verse: *I know for certain that you are bargaining for time* (Daniel 2:8). This new concept of time as a magnitude, like other keystones of the modern world, has buried itself within our consciousness and now masquerades as part of our nature; but it was not always so.

The root is probably ענן, *to appear* or *to present oneself*. As a verb it only shows up in Hebrew in the third construction, where it generally refers to the prohibition against causing spirits to appear. In a certain sense, the closest equivalent to עֵת that we have in English may be the noun *present*, if one takes it in its most literal sense. The present is known by the things that occur or *are presented* in it. Harvest time is marked by our doings in it and by the smell of autumn in the air. Each time has its own character, and through that character we know *the time*.

Our modern notion of time as that which can be ticked off by a clock is more a matter of boredom than of interest. No time seems to have passed by at all when we are having a good time, but time drags on when we have tired and lost all interest. Time as boredom seems to have certain roots in the Newtonian notion of *in-ertia*, that is to say, *artlessness*. Once it was discovered that a body continues to move in a right line even when it has no particular place to go, time must become an endless flow.

אָז

אָז means *then* in either of two senses: (1) referring to that which once was but is no more, or (2) referring to that which is expected, or dreaded or feared.

Before going on with our reading of *Samuel*, a few thoughts are in order concerning the use of a dictionary. When a new word is encountered, the reader must first look for the root. In doing so it is best to bear in mind the classical distinction between *The Letters of the Sun*—those which can appear in roots only—and *The Letters of the Moon*, which may appear either as part of the root, or as one of the additional letters that help to build the form. Letters like ב and ל, even though they may be attached as prepositions, are still considered *Letters of the Sun*.

THE LETTERS OF THE SUN
ב ג ד ז ח ט ל ס ע פ צ ק ר ש

THE LETTERS OF THE MOON
א ה ו י כ מ נ ת

You should consider each individual Letter of the Moon in order to have at your fingertips the various roles each can play when not in the root.

Note that, for the most part, the Letters of the Moon come from the roots הוא, אנת\כ, and מי or מה.

In all dictionaries, verbs in all constructions will be listed under their roots. With regard to nouns, however, dictionaries differ. Some list all nouns under the root; for example, the word מִכְתָּב would probably be found under the root כתב. In other dictionaries, however, the word will be listed under מ. Problems can sometimes arise in the case of words that have irregular or weak roots. Familiarity with the paradigms and the vocalic changes will help narrow down the possibilities; but sometimes one just has to go out on a search.

19. I Samuel 20:13–42

כֹּה־יַעֲשֶׂה יְהֹוָה לִיהוֹנָתָן וְכֹה יֹסִיף כִּי־יֵיטֵב כִּי־אָבִי 13
אֶת־הָרָעָה עָלֶיךָ וְגָלִיתִי אֶת־אָזְנֶךָ וְשִׁלַּחְתִּיךָ וְהָלַכְתָּ
לְשָׁלוֹם וִיהִי יְהֹוָה עִמָּךְ כַּאֲשֶׁר הָיָה עִם־אָבִי׃

The next two verses may be somewhat difficult for the modern
reader. Their complications stem partly from the fact that written
language does not always capture the whole of spoken language.
One problem in Hebrew is that it is often difficult to decide
whether a given string of words is intended as a statement or as a
question. Perhaps the more serious difficulty concerns the word
and. The meaning of *and* in sentences like *He was showing off on
his skis and broke his leg,* or *You mean you were in town and you didn't
call?* is not as simple as it is in the phrase *tea and cookies*. In English
we have a thousand ways of spelling out the word *and*, such as
therefore or *but*, etc., which are rarely used in Hebrew; and so the
range, and hence the ambiguities, in the prefix וֹ are even greater
than in the English *and*. A good author can set the reader up for a
simple *and*, which only in retrospect turns itself into a *but* or even
into an *in spite of the fact that*....

יֹסִיף

The root יסף means *to collect, to add to,* and hence *to continue,* or
to do again. As is the case in many such verbs, the third
construction does not differ much in meaning from the ground
form.

כַּאֲשֶׁר

The word אֲשֶׁר means *that* or *which*, but the role it plays in
Hebrew is somewhat complicated. One can begin to think about
the problem by considering the two English sentences: *This is the
place he spoke of,* and *This is the place that he spoke of*. In English the
difference is not very great, and yet we can feel that the first is a
bit more loosely constructed than the second.

From the beginning Hebrew was, as we have seen, more loosely constructed than English in that notions were placed together rather than being tied together by an *is*. As life and thoughts became more complex only the poets would maintain such fluidity. We can see that clearly in the high prose style of the Book of Job; verse 38:26, for example, reads:

(in it) (no-human) (a wilderness) (no-man) (on-a-land of) (to cause rain)

לְהַמְטִיר עַל־אֶרֶץ לֹא־אִישׁ מִדְבָּר לֹא־אָדָם בּוֹ.

A writer of more common prose, such as one finds in the Book of Genesis, would probably have written מִדְבָּר אֲשֶׁר אֵין אָדָם בּוֹ. The word אֲשֶׁר binds thoughts together and solidifies their interconnection, as in Genesis 1:11:

עֵץ פְּרִי עֹשֶׂה פְּרִי לְמִינוֹ אֲשֶׁר זַרְעוֹ־בוֹ עַל־הָאָרֶץ.

Vocabulary:

עֵץ tree   פְּרִי fruit   מִין kind   זֶרַע seed   אֶרֶץ earth

The word אֲשֶׁר itself appears to be the leaning form of a word אָשֶׁר, but אָשֶׁר does not exist in Hebrew. In Arabic it does exist, and means footstep; while the same word in Akkadian came to mean *there* or *place where*. In the above verse from Genesis one can begin to see the transition. Without the אֲשֶׁר it would have read: *a tree of fruit—it makes fruit to its own kind. Its seed is in it on the earth.* Those who began to add the אֲשֶׁר apparently felt a need to be more explicit about the connection by making the tree be *the place of* the having of the seed. Continual usage then shaped the word into the phrase *by which*. By the time one has verses like the following,

(the firmament) (from under) (which) (the waters) (between) (he divided)

וַיַּבְדֵּל בֵּין הַמַּיִם אֲשֶׁר מִתַּחַת לָרָקִיעַ

the word has become a pronoun.

In English somewhat the same change may have taken place, but in reverse. Consider the two sentences, *This is the house* and *That I saw.* Some say that they were the beginning of our ability to say, *"This is the house that I saw."*

Our word, כַּאֲשֶׁר, can, and often does (as in this case) have its literal meaning: *like that*, as in the sentence *He returned like that* [i.e., *as*] *he said he would.* Most often, however, the word simply means *when*.

14 וְלֹא אִם־עוֹדֶנִּי חָי וְלֹא־תַעֲשֶׂה עִמָּדִי חֶסֶד יְהֹוָה וְלֹא אָמוּת:

עִמָּדִי

עִמָּדִי normally replaces the word עִמִּי. Some scholars think that the change is euphonic, while others think it comes from עִם יָדִי where יד means *hand*.

15 וְלֹא־תַכְרִת אֶת־חַסְדְּךָ מֵעִם בֵּיתִי עַד־עוֹלָם וְלֹא בְּהַכְרִת יְהֹוָה אֶת־אֹיְבֵי דָוִד אִישׁ מֵעַל פְּנֵי הָאֲדָמָה:

וְלֹא־תַכְרִת

The imperative cannot be negated as such. Instead, in this case the imperfect, or hollow state, the state of hopes and fears and expectations is simply denied. The root, כרת belongs to that large cluster of roots centering around the notion of cutting discussed at the end of Chapter Six. This particular root has more a sense of *cutting off*. In this case, the third construction has an intensive rather than a causative sense to it.

עַד־עוֹלָם

עלם is a curious and revealing but perplexing root. In Hebrew it began by meaning *roll up*. From there it developed the meanings *to conceal* and *to be obscure, secret* or *hidden*. At times the root can even mean *to dissemble*, or *to be cunning*. On the other hand, in Arabic it first means *to mark out, to make distinct*, and later it comes to mean *wisdom* or *science*.

One might say that our word עוֹלָם denotes *the great expanse*; it can mean either the whole visible world, or the expanse of all that has been, or all that is expected. מֵעוֹלָם means *forever* and points back to ancient times. לְעוֹלָם and עַד־עוֹלָם mean *forever* and points forward. Like our common use of *forever*, עַד־עוֹלָם more often denotes *till the end*. God will rule עַד־עוֹלָם, but also one person may become the servant of another עַד־עוֹלָם.

We are left, then, with the question of whether the עוֹלָם is so called because it is well marked out and hence open to wisdom and science, or because it is rolled up, obscure, and hidden.

בְּהַכְרִת

בְּהַכְרִת is a noun form of the third construction, founded on the root כרת.

As we already know, the particle בּ can mean *in*, a usage that resembles the Greek dative case. It also shares with the Greek dative the instrumental use, similar to the use of the English word *with* in the admonition, *Don't eat your peas with a knife*. But the word *with* has the smell of a dative in a double sense; for besides the instrumental use just mentioned, it also bears the meaning of *being next to* or *alongside* something. Some moments of reflection are therefore called for. The subject matter of these reflections is of utmost importance because they may concern one of man's earliest attempts to convey the notion of causality, or, to say the same thing, how causality revealed itself to human thought.

Let us begin by looking at the question from the vantage point of Greek by considering the three oblique cases, the genitive, the dative, and the accusative. If we stretch our imaginations, and take words in the largest sense possible, it can be roughly be said that the genitive case implies motion from, the accusative motion to, and the dative absence of motion, or the status of *being with* or *in*. In Hebrew, in Greek, and in English the notion of causality seems to have begun by noting the constant presence of another, either as a בּ, or as a dative, or as a *with*. But how did the early speakers interpret that constant presence? Was it like Humeian conjunction, or was it closer to a feeling of being "in the august presence of..."?

In our verse, the בּ practically comes to mean *when*. The English word "in" displays a similar usage, as in the sentence *In doing A, he accomplished B.*

אֹיְבֵי

This is the plural leaning form of אֹיֵב. The root איב means *enemy*, but it is probably part of that gnarled cluster of roots which includes the root אהב *to love*. Its deepest origins probably lie in the notion of the pure intensity of human feelings.

אִישׁ

The word means *man*, and its plural is אֲנָשִׁים. However, there is another word for *man*, אֱנוֹשׁ, and on occasion one does find a word אִישִׁים. On the other hand, the word for woman which is always paired off with אִישׁ is אִשָּׁה, where the dagesh clearly implies that its root is אנשׁ. The problem, then, is whether our word is from the root אושׁ or the root אנשׁ; and scholars disagree. The first is thought to be related to an Akkadian word for *strong*. The second means *weak, sick*, and when used to describe a wound, it signifies *deadly* or *mortal*. How then does the word אִישׁ look at man? Scholars disagree.

הָאֲדָמָה

The root meaning seems to be *red*. אָדָם is yet another word for *man*, אָדֹם is red, and דָּם is *blood*. Our word אֲדָמָה means *red arable soil*, as opposed to desert. It can be one's own and it can be loved; but unlike the word for *land*, it is totally apolitical in nature.

16 וַיִּכְרֹת יְהוֹנָתָן עִם־בֵּית דָּוִד וּבִקֵּשׁ יְהֹוָה מִיַּד אֹיְבֵי דָוִד:

17 וַיּוֹסֶף יְהוֹנָתָן לְהַשְׁבִּיעַ אֶת־דָּוִד בְּאַהֲבָתוֹ אֹתוֹ כִּי־אַהֲבַת נַפְשׁוֹ אֲהֵבוֹ:

בְּאַהֲבָתוֹ אֹתוֹ

אַהֲבָתוֹ carries a possessive ending (וֹ), which would seem to characterize it as a noun (*his love*). Yet it appears also to have a direct object, אֹתוֹ, which would seem to mark it as a verb. This example reminds us that the distinction between nouns and verbs is derivative and not always fully applicable.

18 וַיֹּאמֶר־לוֹ יְהוֹנָתָן מָחָר חֹדֶשׁ וְנִפְקַדְתָּ כִּי יִפָּקֵד מוֹשָׁבֶךָ:

מוֹשָׁבֶךָ

The root is ישׁב and the form is מַקְטֵל. Table 19.1 on the next page lists some comparable examples.

19 וְשִׁלַּשְׁתָּ תֵּרֵד מְאֹד וּבָאתָ אֶל־הַמָּקוֹם אֲשֶׁר־נִסְתַּרְתָּ שָּׁם בְּיוֹם הַמַּעֲשֶׂה וְיָשַׁבְתָּ אֵצֶל הָאֶבֶן הָאָזֶל:

Root		Noun	
אכל	to eat	מַאֲכָל	food
נתן	to give	מַתָּן	a gift
יצא	to go out	מוֹצָא	an exit
יצע	to lie (recline)	מַצָּע	a bed
ישב	to sit, dwell	מוֹשָׁב	a seat, a dwelling-place

Table 19.1

וְשִׁלַּשְׁתָּ

To do something three times. In the context of this verse, it probably means *you will spend three days*.

תֵּרֵד

The root is ירד, *to go down*.

מְאֹד

Originally מְאֹד meant *force* or *might*. Now if one were to consider a sentence like *They increased מְאֹד upon the land*, one can almost grasp the passage from *might* to *mightily*, where the word has slipped from being a direct object of the verb *increased* to being its modifier. In our verse, מְאֹד modifies the verb ירד, even though it could never have been the verb's direct object. Nonetheless, one can feel the middle ground which made the transition intelligible. Ultimately it comes to mean *exceedingly* or *very much*.

הַמָּקוֹם

Again we have a word of the form מַקְטָל. This time it derives from the root קום, where מָקֹם → מָקוֹם. The root means *to stand, arise,* and hence *to happen*. Just as a מוֹשָׁב (from ישב, *sit*) was a place for sitting, and מַצָּע (from יצע, *recline*) a place for reclining, so מָקוֹם was originally meant a place for standing, *a battle post*, for instance. But then it came to signify the ground of any arising or happening, insofar as that ground has been given its character by that arising. In other words, it means *place*—but always understood to be the place *of something*. Nevertheless, the word has lost all the feeling of having its roots in the notion of standing. Here we can get a good look at *abstracting* at work. It is comparable to what we have seen of the word עת; compare verse 20:12, page 144.

אֵצֶל

The root shows up in Akkadian and in the Arabic וצל, where it means *to join*. In Hebrew the emphasis shifts a bit, first to *take aside*, then to *withdraw* and *take away*, or *to put aside*, although it first meant *to join*.

Our word started off as a noun, *side*. Later it shifted so that the sentence *He is at the side of the altar* became understood as *He is near the altar*—and a preposition, *near*, was born (see page 164).

אֶבֶן

The word means *stone* in most of the Semitic languages, but little more is known about it, though some think the word to be from an Akkadian root *to be sharp*. The phrase הָאֶבֶן הָאָזֶל is apparently a proper noun, but it is mentioned nowhere else.

20 וַאֲנִי שְׁלֹשֶׁת הַחִצִּים צִדָּה אוֹרֶה לְשַׁלַּח־לִי לְמַטָּרָה:

שְׁלֹשֶׁת

A trio (of something). Note that the dot over the second שׁ is doing double duty, both giving the vocalic mode of the ל and distinguishing שׁ from שׂ. This is a fairly common occurrence.

הַחִצִּים

חֵץ, once חִצֵּ (*arrow*) derives from the root חצץ, *to cut in two*. It is part of that large cluster of roots mentioned in the discussion of כרת in verse 20:13.

צִדָּה

The root צדד in Arabic means *to turn aside*. The old form, צַדְּ → צַד, means *side*. Our word, which lightens into צִדָּה, is an old accusative practically turned prepositional.

אוֹרֶה

The root ירה means *to throw* or *to shoot*. The transformation is

$$אַיְרֹה ← אוֹרֶה$$

Here the י becomes ו, as it often does. The ו then goes vocalic, and the ה shortens the רֹ to רֶ.

לְמַטָּרָה:

The dagesh in the ט presents the reader with two possibilities.

Either (a) the form is קְטָלָה, which would make it a noun based on the forceful level of the root מטר, or (b) the form is מַקְטָלָה and the root is נטר—that is, מַטָּרָה ← מַנְטָרָה. That would make the מ a remnant of מִי, giving a noun meaning *who* or *that which does* something. Only a dictionary can help determine which. In cases like this sometimes both words exist as homonyms.

In our case, the root is נטר, meaning *to keep, maintain* or *protect*. The word מַטָּרָה itself means *target* or *mark*. That would make some sense if the word had ever meant something like *shield*; but so far I have found no evidence for that possibility.

21 וְהִנֵּה אֶשְׁלַח אֶת־הַנַּעַר לֵךְ מְצָא אֶת־הַחִצִּים אִם־אָמֹר אֹמַר לַנַּעַר הִנֵּה הַחִצִּים מִמְּךָ וָהֵנָּה קָחֶנּוּ | וָבֹאָה כִּי־שָׁלוֹם לְךָ וְאֵין דָּבָר חַי־יְהוָה:

הַנַּעַר

נער means *lad*. Some suppose an underlying root meaning *to break*, used of the voice, but little is known with clarity.

לֵךְ ... קָחֶנּוּ

The roots הלך, *to go*, and לקח, *to take*, are unique in that they are two of the very few Hebrew words that are irregular in the western sense of the word. That is to say, the irregularity applies to a particular root, and to that root alone, in contrast to the irregularities that arise when certain root letters belongs to certain classes. One would have expected the imperative forms to be לְקַח and הֲלַךְ (since ה cannot accept a simple *shewa*), and indeed, one does have words like לְבַשׁ. But the root לקח is treated as if the ל were a נ; the hollow state is יִקַּח and the imperative is simply קַח. The case of הלך is similar; both roots begin with a somewhat weak letter, and since their imperatives are used frequently, there is a strong tendency to abbreviate them to the two-letter form. The hollow state of הלך is יֵלֵךְ and the imperative is לֵךְ.

22 וְאִם־כֹּה אֹמַר לָעֶלֶם הִנֵּה הַחִצִּים מִמְּךָ וָהָלְאָה לֵךְ כִּי שִׁלַּחֲךָ יְהוָה:

לָעֶלֶם

The word עֶלֶם means *a young man of marriageable age*. It comes from a Semitic root meaning *vigorous*, *lusty*. Except for the feminine form עַלְמָה, there are no other Hebrew words from this root, which is עלם—the Semitic letter ؏ is a totally separate letter from ע and is pronounced like Parisian *R*, that is, as the ג without dagesh was once pronounced in Hebrew.

Here is a fine example of a problem that often arises. We have looked at two separate words that appear to be from the same root: our present word עֶלֶם, and the word עוֹלָם that was discussed in the notes to verse 20:15. In fact, עֶלֶם derives from the root עלם while עוֹלָם is from the root עלם; but since Hebrew does not have the letter ؏ the two roots seem to have collapsed into one.

וָהָלְאָה

הָלְאָה looks like an old accusative turned prepositional, and it means *beyond*. Unfortunately the nominal form never appears, nor does the root exist in a verbal form. However, in Micah 4:7 there is a feminine noun הַנַּהֲלָאָה, which is usually translated *she who was far off*. Since it is a noun based on the first construction, the most reasonable supposition is that the root meant *to be far off*.

23 וְהַדָּבָר אֲשֶׁר דִּבַּרְנוּ אֲנִי וָאָתָּה הִנֵּה יְהוָה בֵּינִי וּבֵינְךָ עַד־עוֹלָם:

24 וַיִּסָּתֵר דָּוִד בַּשָּׂדֶה וַיְהִי הַחֹדֶשׁ וַיֵּשֶׁב הַמֶּלֶךְ עַל [אֶל]־הַלֶּחֶם לֶאֱכוֹל:

25 וַיֵּשֶׁב הַמֶּלֶךְ עַל־מוֹשָׁבוֹ כְּפַעַם | בְּפַעַם אֶל־מוֹשַׁב הַקִּיר וַיָּקָם יְהוֹנָתָן וַיֵּשֶׁב אַבְנֵר מִצַּד שָׁאוּל וַיִּפָּקֵד מְקוֹם דָּוִד:

הַלֶּחֶם

לחם is another one of those roots that splits apart into two nearly opposite meanings. Originally it signified *to be closely packed*. Then it split. Different people reached out in different directions, and yet each could understand the other. For some, *to be closely packed* meant *turmoil* and hence *hand-to-hand combat*; from this branch comes the word מִלְחָמָה or *war*. But people also come together peacefully and share food, and so for others the idea branched off to the most common food available: in Arabic the word came to mean *meat*, in Hebrew, *bread*. Still, compare the seventeenth century use of the word *meat*—and the twentieth century use of the word *bread*.

כְּפַעַם

פַּעַם, another word sometimes translated *time*, is nevertheless quite different from the word עת. It means whatever it is we are counting when we say *once, twice, three times*. The root means *to thrust* (or *hit?*), and it even became the word someone must have reached out for when he saw an anvil for the first time. The root itself means *foot* or *tread*. It also differs from our word *time* (which some say comes from the word *tide*) in that it does not imply regularity.

הַקִיר

The root seems to have a meaning related to *smearing with asphalt*. Our word הַקִיר means *a wall*, or any upright smooth surface of some size.

26 וְלֹא־דִבֶּר שָׁאוּל מְאוּמָה בַּיֹּום הַהוּא כִּי אָמַר מִקְרֶה הוּא בִּלְתִּי טָהֹור הוּא כִּי־לֹא טָהֹור

מְאוּמָה

The dictionary meaning of this word is *something*; but since it is almost always used with a negative its effective meaning is *nothing*. Clearly it is not a root, and some scholars have suggested that it comes from the three words מִי אֹו מָה, but this seems doubtful. More likely is the guess that it comes from the root מאם or מום, meaning *a blemish* or *a spot*. From there it seems to have become *a marked thing* or *a something*, but still having a negative feeling to it.

מִקְרֶה

מִקְרֶה is the closest word in the Bible to the word *chance*. The root is קרה, *to encounter* or *light upon*, and it implies lack of intention. Nevertheless, as is often the case, different books of the Bible see this word differently. Sometimes the fact that something happened by chance mitigates guilt, as in Deuteronomy 23:10:

> If there be among you any man, that is not clean by reason
> of uncleanness that chanceth him by night, then shall he

go abroad out of the camp; he shall not come within the camp.

Sometimes things look as if they might be by chance, but the reader knows they are not; here is I Samuel 6:9:

> And see, if it goeth up by the way of his own coast to Beth-shemesh, then he hath done us this great evil: but if not, then we shall know that it is not his hand that smote us; it was a chance that happened to us.

But for some it is a serious matter, as in Ecclesiastes 9:11:

> I returned, and saw under the sun, that the race is not to the swift, nor the battle to the strong, neither yet bread to the wise, nor yet riches to men of understanding, nor yet favour to men of skill; but time and chance happeneth to them all.

בִּלְתִּי

בִּלְתִּי derives from the root בלת or בלה meaning *to become old and worn out*. Hence the word בְּלִי or בִּלְתִּי—originally meaning *the wearing out of a garment*—later came to mean *the defect or failure of something*, and finally came to mean simply *without*. The ־ִי ending is almost certainly the connective vowel that, as we have seen, the leaning form sometimes requires. It is conceivable, though not likely, that the ־ִי is an old genitive/dative form.

טָהוֹר

In Arabic the root has retained what is probably its original sense, *to remove*. Subsequently, in both Hebrew and Arabic, it came to mean *clean* or *pure*.

27 וַיְהִי מִמָּחֳרַת הַחֹדֶשׁ הַשֵּׁנִי וַיִּפָּקֵד מְקוֹם דָּוִד וַיֹּאמֶר שָׁאוּל אֶל־יְהוֹנָתָן בְּנוֹ מַדּוּעַ לֹא־בָא בֶן־יִשַׁי גַּם־תְּמוֹל גַּם־הַיּוֹם אֶל־הַלָּחֶם

גַּם

The short vocalic mode indicates an original form גַּמְם, from the root גמם. In Arabic that root means *to become abundant*. Our word גַּם is the only word from that root that still exists in Hebrew; it means *also*.

תְּמוֹל

The word is more often found as אֶתְמוֹל. The root is probably תמל. It means *yesterday*, or more generally *some time in the recent past*. Although the word does exist as such in several of the other Semitic languages, to the best of my knowledge nothing else is known about it.

וַיַּעַן יְהוֹנָתָן אֶת־שָׁאוּל נִשְׁאֹל נִשְׁאַל דָּוִד מֵעִמָּדִי 28 עַד־בֵּית לָחֶם:

וַיֹּאמֶר שַׁלְּחֵנִי נָא כִּי זֶבַח מִשְׁפָּחָה לָנוּ בָּעִיר וְהוּא 29 צִוָּה־לִי אָחִי וְעַתָּה אִם־מָצָאתִי חֵן בְּעֵינֶיךָ אִמָּלְטָה נָּא וְאֶרְאֶה אֶת־אֶחָי עַל־כֵּן לֹא־בָא אֶל־שֻׁלְחַן הַמֶּלֶךְ:

צִוָּה

צִוָּה is the forceful level of the ground form. It means *to command* or *to order*, but whatever meaning the ground form itself may have had is not clear.

אָחִי

אָחִי means *brother*, and may or may not go back to a root אחה, *to protect*. It belongs to a strange group of words that includes בֵּן, *son*; אָב, *father*; and חָם, *father-in-law*. Apparently there is a curious and unintelligible rule according to which the names for male relatives have two-letter roots. This rule is so strange as to be suspect. Some scholars take them to be holdovers from what they assume was a much more ancient and primitive stage in the language, in which many if not all roots were two-lettered. However, it is equally possible that אב is part of the cluster of roots that contain the word אהב, *to love*, and that בן is intertwined with בנה *to build*.

אִמָּלְטָה

First person polite imperative of מלט; *to slip away, escape*.

שֻׁלְחַן

The root is the same as the Arabic שלג, a root distinct from the root שלח, which in both Arabic and Hebrew means *to send*.

The Arabic root שלכ means *to strip off a hide*. Our word שֻׁלְחָן is the only Hebrew word deriving from that root; it means *table*. The vocalic mode of the first syllable implies a certain passivity—a stripped-off hide. One might conjecture that the word שֻׁלְחָן goes back to a time when people met and shared their food on hides spread out on the ground. Other examples of this pattern are קָרְבָּן, *an offering*, from the root קרב, *to come near*, and אָבְדָן, *a loss*, from אבד, *to lose*.

30 וַיִּחַר־אַף שָׁאוּל בִּיהוֹנָתָן וַיֹּאמֶר לוֹ בֶּן־נַעֲוַת הַלְוָא יָדַעְתִּי כִּי־בֹחֵר אַתָּה לְבֶן־יִשַׁי לְבָשְׁתְּךָ וּלְבֹשֶׁת עֶרְוַת אִמֶּךָ׃

אַף

This is the word for *nose* mentioned in regard to verse 20:7.

נַעֲוַת

This may be the leaning form of a noun derived from the first construction on the root עוה, which we already know from the word עֲוֹנִי (verse 20:1). Although the reader should be able to figure out what such a form might mean, it is quite a strange form and some people read נַעֲרַת instead; see נַעַר under verse 20:21, above.

הַמַּרְדּוּת

The root מרד means *to rebel*. The feminine ending וּת is often equivalent to our *-ness* or *-hood*. (Recall our earlier remark in Chapter 7 that abstract nouns are often feminine.) Other examples of this form include:

ילד	to give birth	יַלְדוּת	youth
סכל	to be foolish	סִכְלוּת	folly
שבה	to take captive	שְׁבוּת	exile
מלך	to be king	מַלְכוּת	kingdom or royalty
כבד	to be heavy	כְּבֵדוּת	heaviness

הֲלוֹא

As was mentioned earlier, the syntactical difference between a statement and a question is not always clear in Hebrew. On the other hand, it is possible to make a question quite precise by use of the particle הֲ . When it attaches itself to a word it points to it as the center of the question. For example, God asked Adam (Genesis 3:11):

הֲמִן־הָעֵץ אֲשֶׁר צִוִּיתִיךָ לְבִלְתִּי אֲכָל־מִמֶּנּוּ אָכָלְתָּ׃

although He could have asked:

מִן־הָעֵץ אֲשֶׁר צִוִּיתִיךָ לְבִלְתִּי אֲכָל־מִמֶּנּוּ הֶאָכָלְתָּ׃

Our word, הֲלוֹא, is equivalent to *Is it not the case that...?* As in English, the negatively worded question strongly implies a positive answer: *Yes that is the case.* Hence it is often translated *indeed*.

בָּחַר

בחר is an extremely interesting root. Its original meaning was *to catch sight of unexpectedly, to glimpse.* It seems to have been a term connected with hunting, in the sense of catching a glimpse of the game. Its only meaning in Hebrew is *to choose,* though there is often the implication that *the chosen* is *the best*.

The etymology presents a very different picture of choice from the one we have inherited from the mediaeval world of the west. Many of the founders of our western tradition looked at the world in terms of a faculty called the will, an entity to be distinguished from the intellect. But if "hunting" was the paradigm grasped for, the implied thought, conscious or otherwise, may have been that actions are always taken on the basis of limited knowledge or never taken at all. Originally, actions taken in accordance with a mere glance, because of the requirements of time, were said to be done *by a glimpse* or *through choice*. In fact, our own word *choose* goes back to a Gothic word *to perceive* or *to taste*.

לְבָשְׁתְּךָ

The root is בוש, or some close variant. So far as I have been able to discover, its meaning appears to be *shame*—no matter how sophisticated, and hence derivative, the idea of shame may seem to us.

עֶרְוַת

As far as I have been able to determine, the root ערו or ערה has always meant *barren* or *naked,* whether said of a person or of a wasted land.

אִמֶּךָ

The root אמם means *mother*, as it does in so many other languages; some think it may go back to an Akkadian word meaning *wide, roomy*.

31 כִּי כָל־הַיָּמִים אֲשֶׁר בֶּן־יִשַׁי חַי עַל־הָאֲדָמָה לֹא תִכּוֹן אַתָּה וּמַלְכוּתֶךָ וְעַתָּה שְׁלַח וְקַח אֹתוֹ אֵלַי כִּי בֶן־מָוֶת הוּא׃

תִכּוֹן

The root is כון, pretty much identical in meaning to the root קום.

וּמַלְכוּתֶךָ

The root of וּמַלְכוּתֶךָ is מלך; the ending וּת is the same one we saw in הַמַּרְדּוּת.

Note that formally, the word should have been וּמַלְכוּתֶךָ; but perhaps earlier speakers felt that the dagesh would have prevented our ear from picking up the reference to the word מלך.

From the point of view of the first syllable, the shewa is a resting shewa; but from the point of view of the second syllable it is moving and is articulated. Such a shewa is called a *hovering shewa*.

32 וַיַּעַן יְהוֹנָתָן אֶת־שָׁאוּל אָבִיו וַיֹּאמֶר אֵלָיו לָמָּה יוּמַת מֶה עָשָׂה׃

33 וַיָּטֶל שָׁאוּל אֶת־הַחֲנִית עָלָיו לְהַכֹּתוֹ וַיֵּדַע יְהוֹנָתָן כִּי־כָלָה הִיא מֵעִם אָבִיו לְהָמִית אֶת־דָּוִד׃

וַיָּטֶל

The root טול means *to extend*. In some cognate languages, and in later Hebrew as well, the ground form means *to walk about*; but in Biblical Hebrew the root only appears in the third construction, where it means *to hurl*. One might have expected יָטִיל instead, but as you may have noticed from the position of the accent mark, the וּ has shifted the accent forward, lightening the final syllable.

הַחֲנִית

In Hebrew the root חנה means *decline, bend down, encamp*, but in Aramaic it comes to mean *aim*. Our word means *a spear*. The question is whether it is so called because it is *aimed*, or because it was *flexible*.

לְהַכֹּתוֹ

It is not clear what the ground form נכה meant, but the third construction means *to strike*.

34 וַיָּקָם יְהוֹנָתָן מֵעִם הַשֻּׁלְחָן בָּחֳרִי־אָף וְלֹא־אָכַל בְּיוֹם־הַחֹדֶשׁ הַשֵּׁנִי לֶחֶם כִּי נֶעְצַב אֶל־דָּוִד כִּי הִכְלִמוֹ אָבִיו:

נֶעְצַב

The root means *to be sad*.

הִכְלִמוֹ

The root is כלם. The ground form does not exist in Hebrew, but it does in Arabic, where it can mean either *to wound* or *to speak*. In Hebrew it exists in both the first construction, where it means *to feel shame*, and in the third construction, where it means *to put to shame*. The question is whether the Hebrew has somehow combined two distinct sources, or if it is closer to an original meaning which later clove in two, each half traveling far.

35 וַיְהִי בַבֹּקֶר וַיֵּצֵא יְהוֹנָתָן הַשָּׂדֶה לְמוֹעֵד דָּוִד וְנַעַר קָטֹן עִמּוֹ:

בַבֹּקֶר

The root בָּקַר is part of a nest of roots centering about the notion of *splitting*, and split it did; it came to mean *to delve into, to inquire*, later it softened into *to visit*. Another form of the same root is בָּקָר, which refers to *cattle* or *an ox* (because they can pull a plow?). Our word, בֹּקֶר, means *daybreak* or *morning*.

לְמוֹעֵד

The root יעד means *to appoint*. מוֹעֵד is one more interesting view of time. A מוֹעֵד is *a time* because it has been designated as such in advance; compare the English word *appointment*.

36 וַיֹּ֨אמֶר לְנַעֲר֜וֹ רֻ֗ץ מְצָ֥א נָא֙ אֶת־הַ֣חִצִּ֔ים אֲשֶׁ֖ר אָנֹכִ֣י
מוֹרֶ֑ה הַנַּ֗עַר רָ֚ץ וְהֽוּא־יָרָ֥ה הַחֵ֖צִי לְהַעֲבִרֽוֹ׃

לְהַעֲבִרוֹ

This is the third construction on root עבר, *to pass over, go beyond*.

37 וַיָּבֹ֤א הַנַּ֙עַר֙ עַד־מְק֣וֹם הַחֵ֔צִי אֲשֶׁ֥ר יָרָ֖ה יְהוֹנָתָ֑ן
וַיִּקְרָ֨א יְהוֹנָתָ֜ן אַחֲרֵ֤י הַנַּ֙עַר֙ וַיֹּ֔אמֶר הֲל֥וֹא הַחֵ֖צִי
מִמְּךָ֥ וָהָֽלְאָה׃

וַיִּקְרָא

The root קרא means *to call out*.

אַחֲרֵי

The root אחר means *to remain behind.* אַחֵר is the most common word for *other*. Any derivation of the notion of otherness is rather striking, since one would have expected otherness to be one of the ideas most available to human thought. The only reasonable explanation seems to be that otherness only became visible when first one thing, and then another, appeared for someone who could hold the two together in thought even though the other came after the one. Compare the derivation of the word שנים, *two*, from the root שנה, *change* (originally שני; see the discussion on page 50).

The word in our text, אַחֲרֵי is a preposition meaning *after*. It appears to have once been a plural leaning form, as if it originally meant *the followers of...*.

Most scholars agree that except for the monosyllabic prepositions—ל (*to*), ב (*in*), and כ (*like*)—Hebrew prepositions were once either verbs or leaning forms of nouns. In general one can see how the words תַּחַת הָהָר, *the bottom* (a noun) *of the mountain*, might have one day been heard as *under* (a preposition) *the mountain*, or how the simple statement *He climbed* (a verb) *the hill* became the much more sophisticated *He is on* (a preposition) *the hill*. Of prepositions that were once nouns some, like אַחֲרֵי (*after me*), act as if they had once been plural nouns; others, like אֶצְלֵי (*beside me*), act as though they had once been singular.

Even if it should prove impossible to recoup those ancient thoughts which still remain part of us, such scraps as these may help a little to jog some reminiscence of what it meant to participate in the passage from noun to preposition and the dawning of a new way of thought. Here is a list of the more important prepositions with their suggested origins—some certain, others less so. Where it seems appropriate, I include the first person singular ending. I hope I have given readers enough information to allow them to think the transition through; my comments on the examples follow this listing.

to remain behind, delay, tarry	אָחַר
another (proposes one coming behind)	אָחֵר
the hinder parts of ...	אַחֲרֵי
after ...	אַחֲרֵי
be in front of, precede, lead (Arabic only)	אול
to, towards	אֶל, אֵלַי, לְ
be opportune, meet, encounter opportunely	אָנָה
with	אֶת, אִתִּי
lay aside, reserve, withdraw, withhold	אָצַל
join (Arabic)	אצל
conjunction, proximity; beside, next to	אֵצֶל, אֶצְלִי
spend the night (Arabic)	בות
house	בַּיִת
in	בְּ
discern distinguish, observe, mark, give heed to, consider	בִּין
the between of...	בֵּין, בֵּינִי
between	בֵּין, בֵּינִי
to become old and worn out	בָּלָה
a defect of ...	בְּלִי, בִּלְתִּי
without, except	בְּלִי, בִּלְתִּי

to be remote, distant (Arabic)	בעד
away from, behind, about, on behalf of	בְּעַד, בַּעֲדִי, בַּעֲדֵינִי
to be great in rank or dignity	גָּלַל
a great and momentous matter (Arabic)	גלל
on account of…, for the sake of…	בִּגְלַל, בִּגְלָלִי
remove, depart (Arabic)	זול
the removal of…	זוּלַת, זוּלָתִי
except, only, save that	זוּלַת, זוּלָתִי
be firm, set up, established, fixed	כּוּן
right, veritable, honest, thus, so	כֵּן
the like of, like…, as	כְּ
front, in front of	מוּל
conquer, overcome, also: be apparent, conspicuous (Arabic)	נָגַד
(causative) to tell (that is, to make conspicuous)	הִגִּיד
what is conspicuous or in front of…	נֶגֶד, נֶגְדִּי
in front of, in sight of, opposite to	נֶגֶד, נֶגְדִּי
turn about, go around, surround	סָבַב
the parts round about…	סָבִיב, סְבִיבֵי
round about, around	סָבִיב, סְבִיבֵי
to pass over, through, by, to pass on, pass beyond, to overflow	עָבַר
produce, yield	עָבוּר
for the sake of, on account of, in order that	בַּעֲבוּר
to pass on, to advance	עָדָה
perpetuity	עַד
as far as, even to, up to, until, while	עַד

go up, ascend, climb	עָלָה
the heights of…	עַל, עָלַי
upon. on	עַל
be comprehensive, include (Arabic)	עממ
people, peoples, tribes, etc. (probably those united, connected, related)	עַם
with	עִם, עִמִּי
close by, side by side with, parallel to, agreeing with, corresponding to	לְעֻמַּת
answer, respond	עָנָה
(*Does not appear by itself, but only as part of* לְמַעַן *below.*)	(מַעַן)
in response to…, for the sake of, on account of, to the intent of, in order that	לְמַעַן
the under part of…	תַּחַת
under	תַּחַת, תַּחְתִּי

It would be tempting on two counts to suppose that the three monosyllabic prepositions בְּ (*in*), לְ (*to*), and כְּ also have noun origins. First, it would be strange if they and only they among the prepositions had no origin more solid than themselves. Then, too, in each case there is a clear suspect even if there is no complete conviction.

לְ is just a shortened form of אל or על; but the origins of בְּ can only be guessed at. A word found generally in most of the Semitic languages, בית, is normally translated *house*. Actually, it has a somewhat wider meaning, and more accurately denotes the proper place of a thing. While only a person can have a house, all things both animate and inanimate can have a בַּיִת. One might suspect the existence of an older root בית that might have meant *to be in a specific place*, not merely to inhabit. In fact there is a Semitic root בות that means *to spend the night*. Now since ת in the final position, and ו or י in any position are weak letters and liable to drop out, this derivation is at least reasonable. Nevertheless some doubt remains as to whether the root meaning was *to be in a place*, or *to be in one's proper place*. Which interpretation is the more

accurate depends on whether the word בית or the preposition ב
is closer to the original meaning. Unfortunately, there seems to
be little chance of answering this question, since the two
meanings surely diverged well before the invention of writing. In
older times, then, one may have said not *The man is in the field*,
but, so to speak, *The man ins the field*.

As for כְ, a possible origin is the the root כון, which, while it
originally meant *firm* or *upright*, eventually acquires the meaning
set out in order—which is not so far from *a comparison*.

38 וַיִּקְרָא יְהוֹנָתָן אַחֲרֵי הַנַּעַר מְהֵרָה חוּשָׁה אַל־תַּעֲמֹד
וַיְלַקֵּט נַעַר יְהוֹנָתָן אֶת־הַחֵצִי [הַחִצִּים] וַיָּבֹא
אֶל־אֲדֹנָיו׃

מְהֵרָה

מְהֵרָה is the lengthened imperative of the forceful level of the
root מהר. It means *to hasten*. The ground level does not exist in
Hebrew, but in Akkadian it means *to send*. It often occurs along
with another verb, and is usually translated *quickly*.

חוּשָׁה

The root חוש means *to move* in Akkadian, but in Hebrew it
means *to hurry*.

אֲדֹנָיו

In Akkadian the ground form of the root means *to be strong or
firm*. No verb form exists in Hebrew, but there is a noun, אֶדֶן,
that means *a pedestal*. אדון is a term of respect equivalent to
master or *lord*. Our word appears to be a plural of rank referring
to Jonathan, the נַעַר's master. (The plural with the first person
singular possessive ending, אֲדֹנָי, does not denote *my lords*, as
one might have expected, but rather *The Lord*. The same
Akkadian root probably also gave rise to the name *Adonis*.)

39 וְהַנַּעַר לֹא־יָדַע מְאוּמָה אַךְ יְהוֹנָתָן וְדָוִד יָדְעוּ
אֶת־הַדָּבָר׃

40 וַיִּתֵּן יְהוֹנָתָן אֶת־כֵּלָיו אֶל־הַנַּעַר אֲשֶׁר־לוֹ וַיֹּאמֶר לוֹ
לֵךְ הָבֵיא הָעִיר׃

כֵּלָיו

The singular, כְּלִי is much wider than any English equivalent. It can mean *utensil, vessel, garment,* or any small bit of property. In general it seems to refer to any useful man-made object small enough to be carried about. It seems to come from the root כלי, a close kin to כלל (to be complete), which we looked at in verse 20:6; The connection may be that a כלי is a completed object.

41 הַנַּעַר בָּא וְדָוִד קָם מֵאֵצֶל הַנֶּגֶב וַיִּפֹּל לְאַפָּיו אַרְצָה וַיִּשְׁתַּחוּ שָׁלֹשׁ פְּעָמִים וַיִּשְׁקוּ | אִישׁ אֶת־רֵעֵהוּ וַיִּבְכּוּ אִישׁ אֶת־רֵעֵהוּ עַד־דָּוִד הִגְדִּיל:

הַנֶּגֶב

The root נגב means *to be dry* or *parched,* and so it does today in modern Hebrew. But the only form in which the root appears in Biblical Hebrew is the present word נֶגֶב. It means *the dry place* or, more simply put, *south.*

וַיִּפֹּל

The dagesh in the פ shows that the root is נפל, *to fall.*

אַרְצָה

אֶרֶץ is the only word in Hebrew from the root ארץ, but the corresponding Akkadian word is אַרְצְתָ, the Arabic is אַרְד; in German it is *erda,* in Latin *tera,* and in English *earth.* Our form is an old accusative meaning *earthwards.*

וַיִּשְׁתַּחוּ

The root is שחה, *to bow down.* It is a variant of the root שחח, which appears in Akkadian as *oppress.* Our word is in the second construction and means *to bow oneself down.* Note the metathesis between the שׂ and the ת; the word is וַיִּשְׁתַּחוּ rather than וַיִּתְשַׁחוּ as one might have expected. This occurs regularly with sibilants. The regular paradigm of the second construction is given in Table 19.2.

Second Construction (הִתְפָּעֵל)

	Hollow		Solid	
	plur.	sing.	plur.	sing.
3rd masc.	יִתְקַטְּלוּ	יִתְקַטֵּל	הִתְקַטְּלוּ	הִתְקַטֵּל
3rd fem.	תִּתְקַטֵּלְנָה	תִּתְקַטֵּל	הִתְקַטְּלוּ	הִתְקַטְּלָה
2nd. masc.	תִּתְקַטְּלוּ	תִּתְקַטֵּל	הִתְקַטַּלְתֶּם	הִתְקַטַּלְתָּ
2nd fem.	תִּתְקַטֵּלְנָה	תִּתְקַטְּלִי	הִתְקַטַּלְתֶּן	הִתְקַטַּלְתְּ
1st c.	נִתְקַטֵּל	אֶתְקַטֵּל	הִתְקַטַּלְנוּ	הִתְקַטַּלְתִּי

Table 19.2

וַיִּשְּׁקוּ

The root is, of course, נשק. At first it meant *to fasten together*. It then developed into an interesting cluster:

נשא (1)	to lend, to exact usury	נשך	to bite
נשא (2)	to beguile	נשם	to breathe
נשב	to blow	נשף	to blow
נשה	to lend	נשק (1)	to kiss
נשה	to forget	נשק (2)	to arm

רֵעֵהוּ

The root, רעה, is associated with the following cluster:

רעב	to be hungry	רעם	to be violent
רעה (1)	to pasture, rule	רען	to grow luxuriant
רעה (2)	to associate with, be a friend of	רעע (1)	to bake
רעה (3)	to desire	רעע (2)	to be bad or evil

יִבְכּוּ

The root בכה\בכי means *to cry or weep*.

42 וַיֹּאמֶר יְהוֹנָתָן לְדָוִד לֵךְ לְשָׁלוֹם אֲשֶׁר נִשְׁבַּעְנוּ שְׁנֵינוּ
אֲנַחְנוּ בְּשֵׁם יְהוָה לֵאמֹר יְהוָה יִהְיֶה | בֵּינִי וּבֵינֶךָ וּבֵין
זַרְעִי וּבֵין זַרְעֲךָ עַד־עוֹלָם:

בְּשֵׁם

שֵׁם is the word for *name* in most of the Semitic languages.

Some think that it is from the same root as the Arabic ושם, *to brand*, but nothing is known for certain.

Afterword

Now that we reached the end, have we come any closer to the beginning? We have tried in these pages to lay out the foundations for a search. Even if we assume that we have begun to see something of the beginning, the question might still arise, what is that whose beginning we have approached? Perhaps the answer is "the Hebrew language" and perhaps the answer is "the Semitic languages in general." Have we then begun a promising journey back to the beginning of language as such? Perhaps we are not yet in any position to answer such a question.

The Semitic Languages are a very special case. Their closeness to their own beginnings has made it possible to begin the present search with little or no preparatory training. But to raise the question of whether linguistic intentionality always lies behind linguistic formality is to raise a question that can only be answered by the devoted labor of scholars working in many languages.

Our goal is not to discover at last the full range of primitive ideas, but simply to try to rediscover the ancient thoughts which have imperceptibly but relentlessly formed our own speech and our present ways of thinking. Modern linguistics understands its goal to be an account of language as it is understood by those who speak it; that goal presupposes a strict distinction between what is understood and what is not understood, what is felt and what is not felt by the speaker. But if human awareness, feelings and prejudices imperceptibly shade off into the vaguely remembered and the dimly seen, we have no other choice than to try to make the thoughts and half-dead expressions that inhabit the morgue of our minds live again—not because they are true, but because they remain a part of us and yet are only intelligible in their living state.

Postscript (2007)

Some thirty years have gone by since the bulk of this book was written. In the meantime a book much like the one envisioned in the preceding paragraphs has been written. It is one fine book.

Bybee, Joan, Revere Perkins and William Paglucca. *The Evolution of Grammar*. Chicago: University of Chicago Press, 1994.

Sources

The following books were among the most helpful in aiding the author to prepare this volume.

Driver, G. R. *Semitic Writing from Pictograph to Alphabet, revised edition.* Oxford: Oxford University Press (1976)

Gelb, I. J. *A Study Of Writing.* Chicago: University Of Chicago Press

Gesenius, W. et al. *A Hebrew And English Lexicon Of The Old Testament.* Oxford: Oxford University Press (1966)

Jouon, P. Paul, S. J. *Grammaire de L'Hebreu Biblique.* Rome: Institut Biblique Pontifical (1923); also in English as *A Grammar of Biblical Hebrew,* trans. T. Muraoka, 2 vols. (2004).

King, L. W., M.A., F.S.A. *Assyrian Language.* New York: AMS Press (1976)

Koehler, L. and W. Baumgartner. *Lexicon In Veteris Testimenti Libros.* Leiden: E. J. Brill (1958)

Levi-Strauss, Claude. *Structural Anthropology.* New York: Basic Books (1963)

Mallery, Garrick. Picture-Writing of the American Indians. Washington, D.C.: Government Printing Office (1893); reprinted New York: Dover Publications, Inc. (1972)

Moscati, S. et al. *An Introduction to the Comparative Grammar of the Semitic Languages.* Wiesbaden: Otto Harrassowitz, (1969, 1974)

Sperber, Alexander. *Hebrew Grammar, A New Approach.* Jewish Publication Society (1943)

Hebrew Text

POINTED

ספר שמואל א פרק כ

א וַיִּבְרַח דָּוִד מִנָּוֹת [מִנָּיוֹת] בָּרָמָה וַיָּבֹא וַיֹּאמֶר | לִפְנֵי יְהוֹנָתָן מֶה
עָשִׂיתִי מֶה־עֲוֹנִי וּמֶה־חַטָּאתִי לִפְנֵי אָבִיךָ כִּי מְבַקֵּשׁ אֶת־נַפְשִׁי׃
ב וַיֹּאמֶר לוֹ חָלִילָה לֹא תָמוּת הִנֵּה לֹא־יַעֲשֶׂה [יַעֲשֶׂה] אָבִי דָּבָר
גָּדוֹל אוֹ דָּבָר קָטֹן וְלֹא יִגְלֶה אֶת־אָזְנִי וּמַדּוּעַ יַסְתִּיר אָבִי מִמֶּנִּי
אֶת־הַדָּבָר הַזֶּה אֵין זֹאת׃ ג וַיִּשָּׁבַע עוֹד דָּוִד וַיֹּאמֶר יָדֹעַ יָדַע אָבִיךָ
כִּי־מָצָאתִי חֵן בְּעֵינֶיךָ וַיֹּאמֶר אַל־יֵדַע־זֹאת יְהוֹנָתָן פֶּן־יֵעָצֵב וְאוּלָם
חַי־יְהוָה וְחֵי נַפְשֶׁךָ כִּי כְפֶשַׂע בֵּינִי וּבֵין הַמָּוֶת׃ ד וַיֹּאמֶר יְהוֹנָתָן
אֶל־דָּוִד מַה־תֹּאמַר נַפְשְׁךָ וְאֶעֱשֶׂה־לָּךְ׃ ה וַיֹּאמֶר דָּוִד אֶל־יְהוֹנָתָן
הִנֵּה־חֹדֶשׁ מָחָר וְאָנֹכִי יָשֹׁב־אֵשֵׁב עִם־הַמֶּלֶךְ לֶאֱכוֹל וְשִׁלַּחְתַּנִי
וְנִסְתַּרְתִּי בַשָּׂדֶה עַד הָעֶרֶב הַשְּׁלִשִׁית׃ ו אִם־פָּקֹד יִפְקְדֵנִי אָבִיךָ
וְאָמַרְתָּ נִשְׁאֹל נִשְׁאַל מִמֶּנִּי דָוִד לָרוּץ בֵּית־לֶחֶם עִירוֹ כִּי זֶבַח הַיָּמִים
שָׁם לְכָל־הַמִּשְׁפָּחָה׃ ז אִם־כֹּה יֹאמַר טוֹב שָׁלוֹם לְעַבְדֶּךָ וְאִם־חָרֹה
יֶחֱרֶה לוֹ דַּע כִּי־כָלְתָה הָרָעָה מֵעִמּוֹ׃ ח וְעָשִׂיתָ חֶסֶד עַל־עַבְדֶּךָ כִּי
בִּבְרִית יְהוָה הֵבֵאתָ אֶת־עַבְדְּךָ עִמָּךְ וְאִם־יֶשׁ־בִּי עָוֹן הֲמִיתֵנִי אַתָּה
וְעַד־אָבִיךָ לָמָּה־זֶּה תְבִיאֵנִי׃ ט וַיֹּאמֶר יְהוֹנָתָן חָלִילָה לָּךְ כִּי | אִם־יָדֹעַ
אֵדַע כִּי־כָלְתָה הָרָעָה מֵעִם אָבִי לָבוֹא עָלֶיךָ וְלֹא אֹתָהּ אַגִּיד לָךְ׃
י וַיֹּאמֶר דָּוִד אֶל־יְהוֹנָתָן מִי יַגִּיד לִי אוֹ מַה־יַּעַנְךָ אָבִיךָ קָשָׁה׃
יא וַיֹּאמֶר יְהוֹנָתָן אֶל־דָּוִד לְכָה וְנֵצֵא הַשָּׂדֶה וַיֵּצְאוּ שְׁנֵיהֶם הַשָּׂדֶה׃
יב וַיֹּאמֶר יְהוֹנָתָן אֶל־דָּוִד יְהוָה אֱלֹהֵי יִשְׂרָאֵל כִּי־אֶחְקֹר אֶת־אָבִי כָּעֵת
מָחָר הַשְּׁלִשִׁית וְהִנֵּה־טוֹב אֶל־דָּוִד וְלֹא־אָז אֶשְׁלַח אֵלֶיךָ וְגָלִיתִי
אֶת־אָזְנֶךָ׃ יג כֹּה־יַעֲשֶׂה יְהוָה לִיהוֹנָתָן וְכֹה יֹסִיף כִּי־יֵיטִב אֶל־אָבִי
אֶת־הָרָעָה עָלֶיךָ וְגָלִיתִי אֶת־אָזְנֶךָ וְשִׁלַּחְתִּיךָ וְהָלַכְתָּ לְשָׁלוֹם וִיהִי יְהוָה
עִמָּךְ כַּאֲשֶׁר הָיָה עִם־אָבִי׃ יד וְלֹא אִם־עוֹדֶנִּי חָי וְלֹא־תַעֲשֶׂה עִמָּדִי
חֶסֶד יְהוָה וְלֹא אָמוּת׃ טו וְלֹא־תַכְרִת אֶת־חַסְדְּךָ מֵעִם בֵּיתִי
עַד־עוֹלָם וְלֹא בְּהַכְרִת יְהוָה אֶת־אֹיְבֵי דָוִד אִישׁ מֵעַל פְּנֵי הָאֲדָמָה׃
טז וַיִּכְרֹת יְהוֹנָתָן עִם־בֵּית דָּוִד וּבִקֵּשׁ יְהוָה מִיַּד אֹיְבֵי דָוִד׃ יז וַיּוֹסֶף
יְהוֹנָתָן לְהַשְׁבִּיעַ אֶת־דָּוִד בְּאַהֲבָתוֹ אֹתוֹ כִּי־אַהֲבַת נַפְשׁוֹ אֲהֵבוֹ׃
יח וַיֹּאמֶר־לוֹ יְהוֹנָתָן מָחָר חֹדֶשׁ וְנִפְקַדְתָּ כִּי יִפָּקֵד מוֹשָׁבֶךָ׃ יט וְשִׁלַּשְׁתָּ

175

תֵּרֵד מְאֹד וּבָאתָ אֶל־הַמָּקוֹם אֲשֶׁר־נִסְתַּרְתָּ שָּׁם בְּיוֹם הַמַּעֲשֶׂה וְיָשַׁבְתָּ
אֵצֶל הָאֶבֶן הָאָזֶל: כ וַאֲנִי שְׁלֹשֶׁת הַחִצִּים צִדָּה אוֹרֶה לְשַׁלַּח־לִי
לְמַטָּרָה: כא וְהִנֵּה אֶשְׁלַח אֶת־הַנַּעַר לֵךְ מְצָא אֶת־הַחִצִּים אִם־אָמֹר
אֹמַר לַנַּעַר הִנֵּה הַחִצִּים מִמְּךָ וָהֵנָּה קָחֶנּוּ | וָבֹאָה כִּי־שָׁלוֹם לְךָ וְאֵין
דָּבָר חַי־יְהֹוָה: כב וְאִם־כֹּה אֹמַר לָעֶלֶם הִנֵּה הַחִצִּים מִמְּךָ וָהָלְאָה לֵךְ
כִּי שִׁלַּחֲךָ יְהֹוָה: כג וְהַדָּבָר אֲשֶׁר דִּבַּרְנוּ אֲנִי וָאָתָּה הִנֵּה יְהֹוָה בֵּינִי
וּבֵינְךָ עַד־עוֹלָם: כד וַיִּסָּתֵר דָּוִד בַּשָּׂדֶה וַיְהִי הַחֹדֶשׁ וַיֵּשֶׁב הַמֶּלֶךְ עַל
[אֶל] הַלֶּחֶם לֶאֱכֹל: כה וַיֵּשֶׁב הַמֶּלֶךְ עַל־מוֹשָׁבוֹ כְּפַעַם | בְּפַעַם
אֶל־מוֹשַׁב הַקִּיר וַיָּקָם יְהוֹנָתָן וַיֵּשֶׁב אַבְנֵר מִצַּד שָׁאוּל וַיִּפָּקֵד מְקוֹם
דָּוִד: כו וְלֹא־דִבֶּר שָׁאוּל מְאוּמָה בַּיּוֹם הַהוּא כִּי אָמַר מִקְרֶה הוּא
בִּלְתִּי טָהוֹר הוּא כִּי־לֹא טָהוֹר: כז וַיְהִי מִמָּחֳרַת הַחֹדֶשׁ הַשֵּׁנִי וַיִּפָּקֵד
מְקוֹם דָּוִד וַיֹּאמֶר שָׁאוּל אֶל־יְהוֹנָתָן בְּנוֹ מַדּוּעַ לֹא־בָא בֶן־יִשַׁי
גַּם־תְּמוֹל גַּם־הַיּוֹם אֶל־הַלָּחֶם: כח וַיַּעַן יְהוֹנָתָן אֶת־שָׁאוּל נִשְׁאֹל
נִשְׁאַל דָּוִד מֵעִמָּדִי עַד־בֵּית לָחֶם: כט וַיֹּאמֶר שַׁלְּחֵנִי נָא כִּי זֶבַח
מִשְׁפָּחָה לָנוּ בָּעִיר וְהוּא צִוָּה־לִי אָחִי וְעַתָּה אִם־מָצָאתִי חֵן בְּעֵינֶיךָ
אִמָּלְטָה נָּא וְאֶרְאֶה אֶת־אֶחָי עַל־כֵּן לֹא־בָא אֶל־שֻׁלְחַן הַמֶּלֶךְ:
ל וַיִּחַר־אַף שָׁאוּל בִּיהוֹנָתָן וַיֹּאמֶר לוֹ בֶּן־נַעֲוַת הַמַּרְדּוּת הֲלוֹא יָדַעְתִּי
כִּי־בֹחֵר אַתָּה לְבֶן־יִשַׁי לְבָשְׁתְּךָ וּלְבֹשֶׁת עֶרְוַת אִמֶּךָ: לא כִּי כָל־הַיָּמִים
אֲשֶׁר בֶּן־יִשַׁי חַי עַל־הָאֲדָמָה לֹא תִכּוֹן אַתָּה וּמַלְכוּתֶךָ וְעַתָּה שְׁלַח
וְקַח אֹתוֹ אֵלַי כִּי בֶן־מָוֶת הוּא: לב וַיַּעַן יְהוֹנָתָן אֶת־שָׁאוּל אָבִיו וַיֹּאמֶר
אֵלָיו לָמָּה יוּמַת מֶה עָשָׂה: לג וַיָּטֶל שָׁאוּל אֶת־הַחֲנִית עָלָיו לְהַכֹּתוֹ
וַיֵּדַע יְהוֹנָתָן כִּי־כָלָה הִיא מֵעִם אָבִיו לְהָמִית אֶת־דָּוִד: לד וַיָּקָם
יְהוֹנָתָן מֵעִם הַשֻּׁלְחָן בָּחֳרִי־אָף וְלֹא־אָכַל בְּיוֹם־הַחֹדֶשׁ הַשֵּׁנִי לֶחֶם כִּי
נֶעְצַב אֶל־דָּוִד כִּי הִכְלִמוֹ אָבִיו: לה וַיְהִי בַבֹּקֶר וַיֵּצֵא יְהוֹנָתָן הַשָּׂדֶה
לְמוֹעֵד דָּוִד וְנַעַר קָטֹן עִמּוֹ: לו וַיֹּאמֶר לְנַעֲרוֹ רֻץ מְצָא נָא אֶת־הַחִצִּים
אֲשֶׁר אָנֹכִי מוֹרֶה הַנַּעַר רָץ וְהוּא־יָרָה הַחֵצִי לְהַעֲבִרוֹ: לז וַיָּבֹא הַנַּעַר
עַד־מְקוֹם הַחֵצִי אֲשֶׁר יָרָה יְהוֹנָתָן וַיִּקְרָא יְהוֹנָתָן אַחֲרֵי הַנַּעַר וַיֹּאמֶר
הֲלוֹא הַחֵצִי מִמְּךָ וָהָלְאָה: לח וַיִּקְרָא יְהוֹנָתָן אַחֲרֵי הַנַּעַר מְהֵרָה חוּשָׁה
אַל־תַּעֲמֹד וַיְלַקֵּט נַעַר יְהוֹנָתָן אֶת־הַחֵצִי [הַחִצִּים] וַיָּבֹא אֶל־אֲדֹנָיו:
לט וְהַנַּעַר לֹא־יָדַע מְאוּמָה אַךְ יְהוֹנָתָן וְדָוִד יָדְעוּ אֶת־הַדָּבָר: מ וַיִּתֵּן
יְהוֹנָתָן אֶת־כֵּלָיו אֶל־הַנַּעַר אֲשֶׁר־לוֹ וַיֹּאמֶר לוֹ לֵךְ הָבֵיא הָעִיר:
מא הַנַּעַר בָּא וְדָוִד קָם מֵאֵצֶל הַנֶּגֶב וַיִּפֹּל לְאַפָּיו אַרְצָה וַיִּשְׁתַּחוּ שָׁלֹשׁ
פְּעָמִים וַיִּשְׁקוּ | אִישׁ אֶת־רֵעֵהוּ וַיִּבְכּוּ אִישׁ אֶת־רֵעֵהוּ עַד־דָּוִד הִגְדִּיל:
מב וַיֹּאמֶר יְהוֹנָתָן לְדָוִד לֵךְ לְשָׁלוֹם אֲשֶׁר נִשְׁבַּעְנוּ שְׁנֵינוּ אֲנַחְנוּ בְּשֵׁם
יְהֹוָה לֵאמֹר יְהֹוָה יִהְיֶה | בֵּינִי וּבֵינְךָ וּבֵין זַרְעִי וּבֵין זַרְעֲךָ עַד־עוֹלָם:

UNPOINTED

ספר שמואל א פרק כ

א ויברח דוד מנוות [מניות] ברמה ויבא ויאמר | לפני יהונתן מה
עשיתי מה־עוני ומה־חטאתי לפני אביך כי מבקש את־נפשי:
ב ויאמר לו חלילה לא תמות הנה לו [לא] עשה [יעשה] אבי דבר
גדול או דבר קטן ולא יגלה את־אזני ומדוע יסתיר אבי ממני
את־הדבר הזה אין זאת: ג וישבע עוד דוד ויאמר ידע ידע אביך
כי־מצאתי חן בעיניך ויאמר אל־ידע־זאת יהונתן פן־יעצב ואולם
חי־יהוה וחי נפשך כי כפשע ביני ובין המות: ד ויאמר יהונתן
אל־דוד מה־תאמר נפשך ואעשה־לך: ה ויאמר דוד אל־יהונתן
הנה־חדש מחר ואנכי ישב־אשב עם־המלך לאכול ושלחתני
ונסתרתי בשדה עד הערב השלשית: ו אם־פקד יפקדני אביך
ואמרת נשאל נשאל ממני דוד לרוץ בית־לחם עירו כי זבח הימים
שם לכל־המשפחה: ז אם־כה יאמר טוב שלום לעבדך ואם־חרה
יחרה לו דע כי־כלתה הרעה מעמו: ח ועשית חסד על־עבדך כי
בברית יהוה הבאת את־עבדך עמך ואם־יש־בי עון המיתני אתה
ועד־אביך למה־זה תביאני: ט ויאמר יהונתן חלילה לך כי | אם־ידע
אדע כי־כלתה הרעה מעם אבי לבוא עליך ולא אתה אגיד לך:
י ויאמר דוד אל־יהונתן מי יגיד לי או מה־יענך אביך קשה:
יא ויאמר יהונתן אל־דוד לכה ונצא השדה ויצאו שניהם השדה:
יב ויאמר יהונתן אל־דוד יהוה אלהי ישראל כי־אחקר את־אבי כעת
מחר השלשית והנה־טוב אל־דוד ולא־אז אשלח אליך וגליתי |
את־אזנך: יג כה־יעשה יהוה ליהונתן וכה יסיף כי־ייטב אל־אבי
את־הרעה עליך וגליתי את־אזנך ושלחתיך והלכת לשלום ויהי יהוה
עמך כאשר היה עם־אבי: יד ולא אם־עודני חי ולא־תעשה עמדי
חסד יהוה ולא אמות: טו ולא־תכרת את־חסדך מעם ביתי
עד־עולם ולא בהכרת יהוה את־איבי דוד איש מעל פני האדמה:
טז ויכרת יהונתן עם־בית דוד ובקש יהוה מיד איבי דוד: יז ויוסף
יהונתן להשביע את־דוד באהבתו אתו כי־אהבת נפשו אהבו:
יח ויאמר־לו יהונתן מחר חדש ונפקדת כי יפקד מושבך: יט ושלשת
תרד מאד ובאת אל־המקום אשר־נסתרת שם ביום המעשה וישבת
אצל האבן האזל: כ ואני שלשת החצים צדה אורה לשלח־לי
למטרה: כא והנה אשלח את־הנער לך מצא את־החצים אם־אמר
אמר לנער הנה הנה החצים | ממך והנה קחנו | ובאה כי־שלום לך ואין

דבר חי־יהוה: כב ואם־כה אמר לעלם הנה החצים ממך והלאה לך
כי שלחך יהוה: כג והדבר אשר דברנו אני ואתה הנה יהוה ביני
ובינך עד־עולם: כד ויסתר דוד בשדה ויהי החדש וישב המלך על
[אל] הלחם לאכול: כה וישב המלך על־מושבו כפעם | בפעם
אל־מושב הקיר ויקם יהונתן וישב אבנר מצד שאול ויפקד מקום
דוד: כו ולא־דבר שאול מאומה ביום ההוא כי אמר מקרה הוא
בלתי טהור הוא כי־לא טהור: כז ויהי ממחרת החדש השני ויפקד
מקום דוד ויאמר שאול אל־יהונתן בנו מדוע לא־בא בן־ישי
גם־תמול גם־היום אל־הלחם: כח ויען יהונתן את־שאול נשאל
נשאל דוד מעמדי עד־בית לחם: כט ויאמר שלחני נא כי זבח
משפחה לנו בעיר והוא צוה־לי אחי ועתה אם־מצאתי חן בעיניך
אמלטה נא ואראה את־אחי על־כן לא־בא אל־שלחן המלך:
ל ויחר־אף שאול ביהונתן ויאמר לו בן־נעות המרדות הלוא ידעתי
כי־בחר אתה לבן־ישי לבשתך ולבשת ערות אמך: לא כי כל־הימים
אשר בן־ישי חי על־האדמה לא תכון אתה ומלכותך ועתה שלח
וקח אתו אלי כי בן־מות הוא: לב ויען יהונתן את־שאול אביו ויאמר
אליו למה יומת מה עשה: לג ויטל שאול את־החנית עליו להכתו
וידע יהונתן כי־כלה היא מעם אביו להמית את־דוד: לד ויקם
יהונתן מעם השלחן בחרי־אף ולא־אכל ביום־החדש השני לחם כי
נעצב אל־דוד כי הכלמו אביו: לה ויהי בבקר ויצא יהונתן השדה
למועד דוד ונער קטן עמו: לו ויאמר לנערו רץ מצא נא את־החצים
אשר אנכי מורה הנער רץ והוא־ירה החצי להעברו: לז ויבא הנער
עד־מקום החצי אשר ירה יהונתן ויקרא יהונתן אחרי הנער ויאמר
הלוא החצי ממך והלאה: לח ויקרא יהונתן אחרי הנער מהרה חושה
אל־תעמד וילקט נער יהונתן את־החצי [החצים] ויבא אל־אדניו:
לט והנער לא־ידע מאומה אך יהונתן ודוד ידעו את־הדבר: מ ויתן
יהונתן את־כליו אל־הנער אשר־לו ויאמר לו לך הביא העיר:
מא הנער בא ודוד קם מאצל הנגב ויפל לאפיו ארצה וישתחו שלש
פעמים וישקו | איש את־רעהו ויבכו איש את־רעהו עד־דוד הגדיל:
מב ויאמר יהונתן לדוד לך לשלום אשר נשבענו שנינו אנחנו בשם
יהוה לאמר יהוה יהיה | ביני ובינך ובין זרעי ובין זרעך עד־עולם:

Vocabulary List for I Samuel 20
EACH WORD IS DISCUSSED IN THE NOTES
FOLLOWING THE VERSE LISTED

1	אב		1	בקש
19	אבן		1	ברח
15	אדמה		8	ברית
38	אדן		2	גדל
15	אהב		2	גלה
2	או		27	גם
3	אולם		2	דבר
12	אז		13	הלך
2	אזן		2	הנה
29	אח		2	זאת
37	אחר		6	זבח
15	איב		2	זה
2	אין		5	חדש
15	איש		1	חטא
5	אכל		3	חיה
3	אל		2	חלל
6	אם		3	חנן
30	אמם		8	חסד
1	אמר		20	חצץ
30	אף		12	חקר
19	אצל		7	חרה
41	ארץ		26	טהר
13	אשר		7	טוב
1	את		33	טול
1	ב		15	יד
1, 8	בוא		3	ידע
30	בוש		3	יהוה
30	בחר		6	יום
3	בין		13	יסף
1	בית		10	יצא
41	בכה		19	ירד

עין	3	ירה	20
עיר	6	יש	8
על	9	ישב	5
עלם	22	כה	7
עם	5	כון	31
ענה	9	כי	1
עצב	3	כלה	40
ערב	5	כלל	6
ערה	30	כלם	43
עשה	1	כרת	15
עת	12	ל	1
פן	3	לא	2
פנה	1	לחם	6, 24
פעם	25	למה	8
פקד	6	לקח	21
פשע	1	מאד	19
צדד	20	מדוע	2
צוה	29	מה	1
קטן	2	מהר	38
קיר	25	מות	2
קרא	37	מחר	5
קשה	10	מלט	29
רוץ	6	מלך	5
רעה	41	מצא	3
רעע	7	מרד	30
שאל	6	נגב	41
שבע	3	נגד	9
שדה	5	נטר	21
שחה	41	נפל	41
שלח	5	נפש	1
שלם	7	נשק	41
שלש	5	סתר	2
שם	6, 42	עבד	7
שנה	11	עד	5
שפח	6	עוד	3
תמל	27	עוה	1
		עולם	15

Verb Paradigms

I. Ground • Simple Level • Active   (קַל)

	hollow		*solid*	
plural	*singular*	*plural*	*singular*	
יִקְטְלוּ	יִקְטֹל	קָטְלוּ	קָטַל	3rd masc.
תִּקְטֹלְנָה	תִּקְטֹל	קָטְלוּ	קָטְלָה	3rd fem.
תִּקְטְלוּ	תִּקְטֹל	קְטַלְתֶּם	קָטַלְתָּ	2nd masc.
תִּקְטֹלְנָה	תִּקְטְלִי	קְטַלְתֶּן	קָטַלְתְּ	2nd fem.
נִקְטֹל	אֶקְטֹל	קָטַלְנוּ	קָטַלְתִּי	1st c.

	plural		*singular*	
fem.	masc.	fem.	masc.	
קְטֹלְנָה	קִטְלוּ	קִטְלִי	קְטֹל	Imperative
קֹטְלֹת	קֹטְלִים	קֹטֶלֶת	קֹטֵל	Participle

Infinitive
(לְ)קְטֹל

Euphonic transformations:

פ-א	יַאְכֹל ←	יָאכֹל ←	יֹאכַל
פ-ו*	וְסֹב ←	יָסֵב	
	יְוְסֹף ←	יוֹסִף	
	וְסֵב ←	סֵב	
	לְוְסֹף ←	לָסֶפֶת	
פ-י	יְיְטֹב ←	יֵיטֵב	
פ-נ	יְנְגֹש ←	יִגַּשׁ	
פ-ע	יַעֲמֹד ←	יַעֲמֹד	

* Note that Hebrew tends to avoid lexical words beginning with ו (one standard dictionary, consisting of nearly 1200 pages, devotes less than one page to that letter). In the case of a word based on a פ-ו root, when ו is the first letter it transforms to י; otherwise it becomes vocalic.

		קָם	←	קוּם	ע-ו
		יָקוּם	←	יְקֹום	
		יִשְׁחֹט	←	יִשְׁחַט	ע-ח
		בָּן	←	בִּין	ע-י
		סַב	←	סָבַב	ע-ע
סַבּוֹתָ	←	סַבַּאתָ	←	סָבַבְתָּ	
		יַסֹב	←	יִסְבֹב	
		מָצָא	←	מָצָא	ל-א
		יִמְצָא	←	יִמְצֹא	
		יִשָׁח	←	יִשְׁלַח	ל-ח
		גָּלָה	←	גְּלִי	ל-י
		גָּלִיתָ	←	גָּלִיתָ	
		יִגְלֶה	←	יִגְלִי	

II. Ground • Forceful Level • Active (פִּעֵל)

	hollow		*solid*	
	plural	*singular*	*plural*	*singular*	
יְקַטְלוּ	יְקַטֵּל	קִטְּלוּ	קִטֵּל	3rd masc.
תְּקַטֵּלְנָה	תְּקַטֵּל	קִטְּלוּ	קִטְּלָה	3rd fem.
תְּקַטְּלוּ	תְּקַטֵּל	קִטַּלְתֶּם	קִטַּלְתָּ	2nd masc.
תְּקַטֵּלְנָה	תְּקַטְּלִי	קִטַּלְתֶּן	קִטַּלְתְּ	2nd fem.
נְקַטֵּל	אֲקַטֵּל	קִטַּלְנוּ	קִטַּלְתִּי	1st c.

	plural		*singular*	
	fem.	masc.	fem.	masc.	
קַטֵּלְנָה	קַטְּלוּ	קַטְּלִי	קַטֵּל	Imperative
מְקַטְּלֹת	מְקַטְּלִים	מְקַטֶּלֶת	מְקַטֵּל	Participle

Infinitive
(לְ)קַטֵּל

Euphonic transformations:

קוֹמֵם	←	קֵוֹם	ע־ו
סוֹבֵב	←	סְבֵב	ע־ע
בֵּרֵךְ	←	בִּרֵךְ	ע־ר
יְבָרֵךְ	←	יְבִרֵךְ	
מִצֵּאתָ	←	מִצְאֵתָ	ל־א
גִּלָּה	←	גִּלֵי	ל־י
שִׁלַּח	←	שִׁלֵּח	ל־ח

III. Ground • Forceful Level • Passive   (פֻּעַל)

hollow		*solid*		
plural	*singular*	*plural*	*singular*	
יְקֻטְלוּ	יְקֻטַּל	קֻטְּלוּ	קֻטַּל	3rd masc.
תְּקֻטַּלְנָה	תְּקֻטַּל	קֻטְּלוּ	קֻטְּלָה	3rd fem.
תְּקֻטְּלוּ	תְּקֻטַּל	קֻטַּלְתֶּם	קֻטַּלְתָּ	2nd masc.
תְּקֻטַּלְנָה	תְּקֻטְּלִי	קֻטַּלְתֶּן	קֻטַּלְתְּ	2nd fem.
נְקֻטַּל	אֲקֻטַּל	קֻטַּלְנוּ	קֻטַּלְתִּי	1st c.

plural		*singular*		
fem.	masc.	fem.	masc.	
–	–	–	–	Imperative
מְקֻטְּלֹת	מְקֻטְּלִים	מְקֻטֶּלֶת	מְקֻטָּל	Participle

Infinitive

(לְ)קֻטַּל

Euphonic transformations:

בֹּרַךְ	←	בֻּרַּךְ	ע-ר
מֻצָּא	←	מֻצָּא	ל-א

IV. First Construction • Simple Level • Reflexive-Passive (נִפְעַל)

hollow*		solid		
plural	*singular*	*plural*	*singular*	
יִקָּטְלוּ	יִקָּטֵל	נִקְטְלוּ	נִקְטַל	3rd masc.
תִּקָּטֵלְנָה	תִּקָּטֵל	נִקְטְלוּ	נִקְטְלָה	3rd fem.
תִּקָּטְלוּ	תִּקָּטֵל	נִקְטַלְתֶּם	נִקְטַלְתָּ	2nd masc.
תִּקָּטֵלְנָה	תִּקָּטְלִי	נִקְטַלְתֶּן	נִקְטַלְתְּ	2nd fem.
נִקָּטֵל	אֶקָּטֵל	נִקְטַלְנוּ	נִקְטַלְתִּי	1st c.

* Note that in the hollow state the נ is devoured by the ק, but its echo is still present as the dagesh in the ק.

plural		*singular*		
fem.	masc.	fem.	masc.	
הִקָּטֵלְנָה	הִקָּטְלוּ	הִקָּטְלִי	הִקָּטֵל	Imperative
נִקְטָלֹת	נִקְטָלִים	נִקְטָלָה	נִקְטָל	Participle

Infinitive

(לְ)הִקָּטֵל

Euphonic transformations:

נֶאֱכַל	←	נִאֲכַל	פ-א
יֵאָכֵל	←	יִאָכֵל	
נוֹסַף	←	נִוְסַף	פ-ו
נִגַּשׁ	←	נִנְגַּשׁ	פ-נ
נֶעֱמַד	←	נִעֲמַד	פ-ע
יֵעָמֵד	←	יִעֲמֵד	
נָקוֹם	←	נִקְוֹם	ע-ו
נִשְׁחֲטוּ	←	נִשְׁחְטוּ	ע-ח
נָדוֹן	←	נִדְיַן	ע-י

נָסַב	←	נִסְבַב	ע-ע
נְסַבּוֹתָ	←	נִסְבַּבְתָּ	
יִסַּב	←	יִסָּבֵב	
נִמְצָא	←	נִמְצָא	ל-א
נִמְצֵאתָ	←	נִמְצָאתָ	
תִּמָּצֶאנָה	←	תִּמָּצֶאנָה	
יִשָּׁלַח	←	יִשָּׁלֵח	ל-ח
נִגְלָה	←	נִגְלַי	ל-י
יִגָּלֶה	←	יִגָּלֵי	

V. Second Construction • Forceful Level •
Reciprocal-Reflexive   (הִתְפַּעֵל)

	hollow			solid		
	plural	*singular*		*plural*	*singular*	
	יִתְקַטְּלוּ	יִתְקַטֵּל		הִתְקַטְּלוּ	הִתְקַטֵּל	3rd masc.
	תִּתְקַטֵּלְנָה	תִּתְקַטֵּל		הִתְקַטְּלוּ	הִתְקַטְּלָה	3rd fem.
	תִּתְקַטְּלוּ	תִּתְקַטֵּל		הִתְקַטַּלְתֶּם	הִתְקַטַּלְתָּ	2nd masc.
	תִּתְקַטֵּלְנָה	תִּתְקַטְּלִי		הִתְקַטַּלְתֶּן	הִתְקַטַּלְתְּ	2nd fem.
	נִתְקַטֵּל	אֶתְקַטֵּל		הִתְקַטַּלְנוּ	הִתְקַטַּלְתִּי	1st c.

	plural		*singular*		
	fem.	masc.	fem.	masc.	
	הִתְקַטֵּלְנָה	הִתְקַטְּלוּ	הִתְקַטְּלִי	הִתְקַטֵּל	Imperative
	מִתְקַטְּלֹת	מִתְקַטְּלִם	מִתְקַטֶּלֶת	מִתְקַטֵּל	Participle

Infinitive
(לְ)הִתְקַטֵּל

Euphonic transformations:

הִתְבָּרֵךְ	←	הִתְבָּרֵךְ	ע-ר
הִתְמַצֵּאתִי	←	הִתְמַצֵּאתִי	ל-א
הִשְׁתַּלַּח*	←	הִתְשַׁלַּח	ל-ח
הִתְגַּלֵּה	←	הִתְגַּלֵּי	ל-י

*Note that in the case of a sibilant like שׁ or שׂ or ס, the sibilant and the ת euphonically interchange.

VI. Third Construction • Simple Level • Active   (הִפְעִיל)

| hollow | | solid | | |
plural	singular	plural	singular	
יַקְטִילוּ	יַקְטִיל	הִקְטִילוּ	הִקְטִיל	3rd masc.
תַּקְטֵלְנָה	תַּקְטִיל	הִקְטִילוּ	הִקְטִילָה	3rd fem.
תַּקְטִילוּ	תַּקְטִיל	הִקְטַלְתֶּם	הִקְטַלְתָּ	2nd masc.
תַּקְטֵלְנָה	תַּקְטִילִי	הִקְטַלְתֶּן	הִקְטַלְתְּ	2nd fem.
נַקְטִיל	אַקְטִיל	הִקְטַלְנוּ	הִקְטַלְתִּי	1st c.

| plural | | singular | | |
fem.	masc.	fem.	masc.	
הַקְטֵלְנָה	הַקְטִילוּ	הַקְטִילִי	הַקְטֵל	Imperative
מַקְטִילֹת	מַקְטִילִים	מַקְטִילָה	מַקְטִיל	Participle

Infinitive

(לְ)הַקְטִיל

Euphonic transformations:

	←		
הֶאֱכִיל	←	הַאֲכִיל	פ-א
הוֹשִׁיב	←	הֻוְשִׁיב	פ-ו
הֵיטִיב	←	הַיְטִיב	פ-י
הִגִּישׁ	←	הַנְגִּישׁ	פ-נ
הֶעֱמִיד	←	הַעְמִיד	פ-ע
הֵקִים	←	הַקְוִים	ע-ו
הֵסֵב	←	הַסְבִיב	ע-ע
הִמְצֵאתָ	←	הִמְצַאְתָ	ל-א
הִשְׁלִיחַ	←	הַשְׁלִיח	ל-ח
הִגְלָה	←	הִגְלְיי	ל-י
הִגְלֵיתָ	←	הִגְלַיְתָ	

VII. Third Construction • Simple Level • Passive (הֻפְעַל)

	hollow		solid		
	plural	*singular*	*plural*	*singular*	
	יֻקְטְלוּ	יֻקְטַל	הֻקְטְלוּ	הֻקְטַל	3rd masc.
	תֻּקְטַלְנָה	תֻּקְטַל	הֻקְטְלוּ	הֻקְטְלָה	3rd fem.
	תֻּקְטְלוּ	תֻּקְטַל	הֻקְטַלְתֶּם	הֻקְטַלְתָּ	2nd masc.
	תֻּקְטַלְנָה	תֻּקְטְלִי	הֻקְטַלְתֶּן	הֻקְטַלְתְּ	2nd fem.
	נֻקְטַל	אֻקְטַל	הֻקְטַלְנוּ	הֻקְטַלְתִּי	1st c.

plural		*singular*		
fem.	masc.	fem.	masc.	
–	–	–	–	Imperative
מֻקְטְלֹת	מֻקְטָלִים	מֻקְטָלָה	מֻקְטָל	Participle
		לְהֻקְטַל	–	Infinitive

Infinitive

(לְ)הֻקְטַל

Euphonic transformations:

הָאֳכַל	← הָאֳכַל	פ-א
הֻגַּשׁ	← הָנְגַּשׁ	פ-נ
הָעֳמַד	← הָעֳמַד	פ-ע
הוּסַב	← הָסֳבַב	ע-ע
הֻמְצָא	← הָמְצָא	ל-א
הֻגְלָה	← הָגְלִי	ל-י

Index

W

Y

About the Author

Robert D. Sacks was born 1931 in Akron, Ohio, where he would spend Saturdays with his grandfather in an old synagogue that stood on grounds now occupied by the United Disability Service. He continued his education at St. John's College, Annapolis, Maryland, (B.A. 1954), and at The Johns Hopkins University (Ph.D. 1961). In the intervening years he studied with Leo Strauss, first at the Hebrew University, Jerusalem and later at the University of Chicago. In 1957 he enrolled at the Ecole des Langues Orientales Vivantes in Paris but admits having spent most of his days at the Café de la Rue Tournould. Sacks has taught at St. John's College since 1960, at both the Annapolis and the Santa Fe campuses.

Robert Sacks is the author of two previous books: *A Commentary on the Book of Genesis* (Edwin Mellen Press, 1990) and *The Book of Job with Commentary: A Translation for Our Time* (Scholars Press, 1999).